ASK Leading Women™

No Ceiling,
No Walls

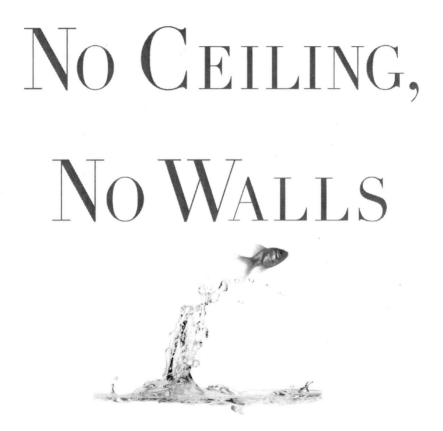

*What women haven't been told
about leadership from career-start
to the corporate boardroom.*

Susan L. Colantuono
CEO and Founder, Leading Women

For information on reprints and/or bulk orders, contact:
Permissions
Interlude Productions
PO Box 1124
Charlestown, RI 02813
USA
1-401-789-0441

Cover and Interior Design: 1106 Design, www.1106design.com

Book Cover Text: Graham Van Dixhorn and Susan Kendrick, Write for Your Market, Inc.

Editing and copy editing: The Baldwin Group, Dallas, TX (Juli@BaldwinGrp.com)

Printed in the United States of America
14 13 12 11 10   5 4 3 2 1

Library of Congress Cataloging-in-Publication Data

Colantuono, Susan Lee
      No Ceiling, No Walls: What women haven't been told about leadership from career-start to the corporate boardroom / Susan L. Colantuono
      p. cm.
ISBN 978-0-9673129-2-7
1. Leadership 2. Women executives 3. Leadership in women 4. Management
I. Colantuono, Susan Lee II. Title III. What women haven't been told about leadership from career-start to the corporate boardroom
HD6054.3.C65 2010
658.4'092'082—dc22
                        2009910227

Advance Praise for *No Ceiling, No Walls*

"Women of all ages and career levels must incorporate the ideas in this thoughtful book on leadership. The future depends on women acknowledging that there is nothing holding them back from succeeding in business."

— VICKI DONLAN, AUTHOR
HER TURN: WHY IT'S TIME FOR WOMEN TO LEAD IN AMERICA

"Colantuono's book provides thoughtful coaching to women leaders, whether experienced or new to the workforce. Her wise and practical advice is a must-read for individuals who are determined to reach the next level of their careers."

— ANNE SZOSTAK, PRESIDENT & CEO OF SZOSTAK PARTNERS AND
FORMER CHAIRMAN AND CEO, FLEET BANK RHODE ISLAND

"Informed by her extensive experience, Susan Colantuono offers a refreshingly keen, sophisticated analysis of what women need to do to become leaders. This is a must-read book for women and men who want more women in leadership positions in America."

— EVELYN MURPHY, AUTHOR
*GETTING EVEN: WHY WOMEN DON'T GET PAID
LIKE MEN AND WHAT TO DO ABOUT IT*

Praise from participants of
No Ceiling, No Walls live programs

"Within a year of completing the program, I was promoted (value $25K). I live by what you taught and have not stopped training and learning new skills to become a savvier leader."

"…when my boss asked again, 'What do you want to do next?' I was direct. I want to manage managers, if not here then somewhere else by the end of the year. Within three months I was promoted to Director. My SVP called me into his office to tell me that he'd seen a significant improvement in my 'business acumen' (his words). The program was money VERY well spent!"

"The benefits of the program last a career lifetime. I attended three years ago and learned a great deal about power, presence and presentation. I was asked to deliver a career-altering presentation to a national audience this spring. I knocked it out of the park due to what I learned in the program."

"Attending the program made me a more courageous leader. I am able to stay true to myself, while working the strategic and political networks within my company."

"I am a great deal more confident. I keep the workbook next to my desk and refer to it when pondering something I can't get my arms around. The course was an extremely positive and motivating experience. I completely refined and became more cognizant of my leadership skills."

"I'm more aware of the image I'm projecting and how I was being perceived, as opposed to how I wanted to be perceived. I learned important but relatively simple ways to improve that. I have to tell you, there isn't a day (or event) that goes by that I don't find myself using the tools, techniques and strategies I learned in your program!"

"Learning to develop and use a strategic network has been invaluable. I never understood what it meant and lost countless opportunities because I didn't feel comfortable connecting strategically with people."

All *ASK Leading Women*™ books offer inspiring and
practical solutions for women as they move from career-start
to the C-suite and onto corporate boards. When you
ASK Leading Women, you get cutting-edge content,
ready-to-apply tools, insights from self-assessments, and
examples from successful women who act as your virtual mentors.

Other Books by Susan Colantuono

Build Your Career: Getting Ahead Without Getting Out

Make Room for JOY: Finding Magical Moments in Your Everyday Life

Dedication

With love and appreciation for the support and love of Mom and Dad without whom I wouldn't have lived a life "in the lead" of my six siblings!

To my sibs, Tom, Nancy, Janet, Lynn, Ann and David, who put up with my first-born position of leadership. Special thanks to my brother Tom, who came along 16 months after I was born to teach me about gender dynamics and who, with my brother Dave, were idolized by our Nana as "Tommy-boy" and "Davey-boy."

To my son Justin and his seven female cousins — may you each have meaningful lives and careers with no ceiling and no walls.

In memory of Nana and Gramma — feisty, proud and strong women both. And Da, who loved us all unconditionally.

I love you one and all.

Table of Contents

No Ceiling, No Walls

*"We read books to find out who we are. What other people, real
or imaginary, do and think and feel is an essential guide to our
understanding of what we ourselves are and may become."*
—Ursula K. Le Guin, author

This book is for you if you…
- Believe that the playing field has been leveled and women are as likely to advance as men.
- Need a mid-course correction because your career has stalled.
- Take leadership development courses from your organization and expect them to help you climb the corporate ladder.
- Wonder why a man got the job you thought you were perfect for.
- Can't believe that your excellent interpersonal skills haven't propelled you up the organization.
- Believe in the idea that *leadership* is different than *management* — and think it will help you succeed.
- Can't read a financial report…and don't think it really matters.
- Think that the path upward is deeper professional expertise.
- Think that you are paid to do your job.

○ Think that *what* you say is more important than *how* you say it.
○ Are at career-start and want to get off on the right foot.
○ Need to know what it means to lead at the middle- or senior-management level.
○ Wonder what it takes to succeed at the executive level.
○ Hope to serve on not-for-profit or for-profit boards.

In other words, if you have unrealized career goals, within these pages you'll gain insights that will help you reframe your thinking and move beyond obstacles in order to achieve your goals.

Succeeding "Outside the Box"

To become the best leader you can be, you will have to succeed outside the box that we've been *told* constrains women. Since the mid-'80s we've heard about the *glass ceiling* that holds women down. In the early '90s, we were introduced to the concept of *maternal walls* that fence us in with negative stereotypes about mothers' lack of commitment to careers (and appropriateness in the workplace). And we've learned about the *sticky floor* — that collection of personal weaknesses that can hold women at the bottom. In other words, we're described as boxed in — ceiling, walls and floor.

Don't misunderstand. I acknowledge the reality of the barriers. Some of our own attitudes and behaviors impede our aspirations (sticky floor); many of us encounter stereotypes that get in the way of career progress and wage equity (glass ceiling); and some women work in mother-hostile organizational cultures that block advancement (maternal wall).

But I'm sure you'd agree that being "boxed in" doesn't describe the career that you want. You might see obstacles, but you don't want to give them power. While you might temporarily feel discouraged by a bump in the road, you want to use your purpose, power and presence to overcome it. You're on a career path, and you want to take the next step.

But to take that next step, there are some things you need to know. First, any step up the ladder will depend solely on your leadership abilities. Second, that next step can seem so daunting, and perhaps even unattainable, because of the important things about leadership that you — and other women like you — haven't been told.

What Women Haven't Been Told...

In 1999, I was called back to an early interest — to focus on powering the success of women by helping them become more effective leaders. Knowing that women are consistently viewed as outperforming men in most skills and attributes traditionally associated with leadership, I turned my attention to these questions:

> **If we (women) are so good, why are there so few of us at the top?**

> **Why aren't there more of us in senior positions when we tend to have a natural advantage in terms of interpersonal skills?**

> **Why, when there's been such great advice offered in books for women, isn't our progress faster?**

Sure, there are still stereotypes that block advancement. Sure, we limit ourselves in some ways. Sure, some cultures, policies and programs put us at a disadvantage. But what if that's not all, I asked. Is there something else? Is there something that women aren't being told?

The answer is yes.

You see, nearly everything we've been told about leadership for the last 30 years has been based on research on *men*. The most outstanding noticeable attributes of successful male executives is their interpersonal skills because that is an area of weakness for most men. Career advice derived from this research states that one needs to be professionally competent and have excellent interpersonal skills to progress up the corporate ladder.

What is unsaid is that one also must have excellent **business skills.** It's the "fish in water" syndrome: A fish doesn't know it's in water until it's pulled out into the air. Leadership gurus don't realize that business skills are crucial because these skills are *assumed.* Successful male leaders tend to have strong business, strategic and financial acumen. That's not what sets them apart. What sets them apart is their interpersonal skills.

So while the traditional leadership success equation involves professional competence and interpersonal skills, there is actually a third factor — business skills — that has been "hidden." Both men and women have been told about only two-thirds of the success equation. Men either have the third part (business skills) naturally, or they are selected for management training experiences where they are coached or mentored in business acumen.

Many women aren't even aware that there is a third part to the equation. We feel so proud when our staff loves us, not realizing that those above us are asking, "Great, but what have you done for the business today?" We're blindsided when an executive says to us, "You're so nice, but are you effective?" Or we believe that if we are but our authentic selves, our career success will be guaranteed.

This discovery — that **women haven't been told about 33% of the leadership success equation and therefore are missing it in their quest for leadership success** — became the foundation of my work. I've seen the profound impact this discovery has had on the lives of hundreds of women — some of whose testimonials are in the front of this book. They have more confidence in their leadership. They network more strategically. They are seen as more credible businesswomen. They have been promoted or received more challenging assignments. They are more courageous. They present with greater impact and poise.

I wrote *No Ceiling, No Walls* to extend these impacts to women like you. In it you'll find something that will help you move to the next level — if not in your current organization, then in another. If you hope to understand leadership at the next highest level, you will. If you need to figure out how to network more strategically, you will.

If you expect to acquire business acumen, you will. If you want to enhance your leadership presence, you will.

...And Why I'm Telling You

Chances are pretty good that I've been where you are. Undoubtedly, I have worked with people who are where you are. My career has spanned every organizational level. Starting as an individual contributor, I moved into a project lead position before becoming a supervisor and then manager. I left corporate life to become a solopreneur and then an executive in boutique consulting firms. Now I am CEO of my own business.

From 1974 to 1979, I was a manager and I taught management skills at Connecticut General Life Insurance Company (now CIGNA). For the next 20 years through my consulting practice, I not only held other leadership positions, I also saw leadership in action as I worked with managers and executives on complex change. I've managed multimillion-dollar global projects and worked with managers and executives of all stripes and both genders. I've worked in or consulted to small not-for-profits, large national companies and Fortune 50 global companies in nearly every industry sector. Some of my managers and consulting clients were superb leaders; others were not. Each manager or client taught me something about leadership.

Through this variety of leadership positions and relationships with those in leadership positions, I learned from my own and others' successes. I also learned from my dismal failures. Like you, I have faced challenges that are independent of gender, and I have faced challenges specific to women. I remember "Bob," who told me I was too emotional. I've pitched new business ideas — and not been taken seriously. When a male peer caught the boss' ear and reorganized the department, I ended up reporting to him. Ideas I presented were credited to men who recycled them at the same meeting. When I think of these challenges, I find myself wishing I knew then what I'm going to share with you in the pages of this book.

Through it all, though sometimes on the front burner and sometimes on the back, my commitment to women's advancement never wavered.

In the early '70s, Priscilla Kania, Pat Minicucci and I launched one of the first women's initiatives in the country in an effort to address stereotypes about women and to correct policies and programs that put women at a disadvantage in advancement and pay equity. Within 3 years, our efforts helped increase the percentage of women first-line supervisors from 9% to 23% and women officers from 3 percent to 7.5%. We caused vacant positions to be posted instead of filled in "smoky back rooms." And we helped open the first on-site day-care center in the country.

Eventually, I founded Leading Women, an organization that is 100% committed to helping women advance in their careers and helping organizations advance the women who work in them. I guide overall strategy and work with amazing women who run our local affiliates. Together we work to inspire, power and honor the success of women leaders in organizations and strengthen and align women's initiatives, networks and affinity groups.

I once read a quote that went something like this: *You are called to the place where your deep gladness meets the world's deep hunger.* I believe that Leading Women is the fulfillment of that calling for me. I believe that my profession chose me. It enables me to reach out and support the success of other women — through mentoring relationships, live presentations and resources like this book.

Your Role Models and Virtual Mentors

However, you don't have to rely on just my word. Within these pages, you'll meet many amazingly successful women whose experiences and advice reinforce what it is that women need to know about leadership but haven't been told.

Many of the women who will act as role models and virtual mentors are Fortune 500 women CEOs. Why? Because climbing to the top of an F500 company is arguably the hardest career path there is — especially for a woman — and these women have made it against all odds, in vastly different industries and in many that are heavily male.

Never before have there been so many women CEOs of F500 companies. As I write, there are 15. Their successes make it an exhilarating time for you because their diversity demonstrates that there is no one "right way" to build a career, no single mold you have to fit and no implicit message that you have to be like so-and-so or be like a man to get to the top. This variety makes it easy to learn from the experiences and wisdom of these women and others. While they don't prescribe a single path to success, their experiences, philosophies and advice do suggest important common lessons.

Some of these accomplished women have achieved and sustained extraordinary outcomes for their businesses. For example, at the end of 2008, after a remarkable turn around, Xerox stock had a net increase under Anne Mulcahy's reign; Avon's had grown more than 65% under Andrea Jung; and Susan Ivey had increased Reynolds American's by more than 20%. Although other women CEOs have not fared as well with their outcomes, they have equally important lessons to teach.

While the titles and companies of the featured women were accurate at the time their stories or quotes were written, things change, and when you read this book there might be some who have gone on to new opportunities. Regardless, they are still powerful mentors. They will give you an inside glimpse into what real women leaders do, think and feel.

If you wonder why most of the women highlighted in this book are CEOs, it's not because I'm suggesting that you have to aspire to be a CEO (although it's great if you do). You can learn from these women no matter your specific goals, because the skills they've acquired are the same skills you need to move up, no matter your current level. They've likely had a job at the same level as yours…and they've successfully moved beyond it. So, unless you're happy right where you are (if so, why'd you pick up this book?), you can use the leadership, career and life lessons of these women to power your success.

Getting the Most from this Book

No Ceiling, No Walls will give you a better understanding of who you are as a leader and the leader you may become. It's not a book you will breeze through on a plane ride or finish in a weekend. It is intended to be a guide to the missing elements of leadership for women. Think of it like a college course. Give yourself several months (a "semester," if you will) to read it, re-read it, digest the material, complete the activities and, most importantly, practice your new skills.

The book is divided into two sections. In Part One, you'll learn why leadership is *the* critical success factor for career advancement and you'll learn why you should be wary of (or even ignore) much conventional wisdom about leadership. When you've completed this section, you will have learned 21 lessons in leadership that women are rarely told but need to know in order to be successful. To help cement these important messages, each is highlighted in the "Lessons in Leadership" section at the end of each chapter.

Part Two focuses on concrete and specific skills and knowledge you can (and must) learn in order to achieve your career goals. In particular, it focuses on areas where women are consistently perceived as underperforming men. You'll be introduced to seven leadership skills that are seldom taught and *why* they're essential. You'll learn how four essential leadership skills differ by level and how to master them at every level. And you'll discover what your positional purpose is and *why* you have to know it in order to lead.

Within the Lead ON!™ sections at the end of each chapter you will find self-assessments, practical solutions and ready-to-apply tools. These will help you develop the skills you need to be a more effective leader — no matter the level you are today. They won't guarantee success, but failing to master them *will* guarantee your career is boxed in.

By reading this book and using the Lead ON! tools, you'll power up your leadership skills for career success. You'll find the courage, skills and inspiration to bust out of any box that has kept you confined. Now, to create your No Ceiling and No Walls career...read on!

PART ONE

What Women Haven't Been Told About Leadership

Beware of Conventional Wisdom

"Each of us can practice what CEOs with superb business acumen do instinctively: cut through all the clutter using the universal laws of business, and select the right business priorities... Whether you're a CEO, the head of a department, or someone just starting [her] career, you must be a leader of the business and a leader of people. A leader of the business knows what to do. A leader of people knows how to get it done..."

—RAM CHARAN
WHAT THE CEO WANTS YOU TO KNOW

Several years ago when I was called to focus on powering the success of women by helping them become more effective leaders, I realized that I needed a new definition of leadership. To effectively learn a concept as important as *leadership*, women need to be on the same page.

Conventional wisdom about leadership leads people astray. There is an astonishing number of definitions of leadership — many focusing on different things. Not only is there great variance among definitions, there are problems with many of them. Let's take, for example, the fundamental idea that a leader is someone with followers. Well, unless you're comfortable being lumped in with Hitler or Osama bin Laden, that definition is useless and not prescriptive.

3

The definition that "leadership is action, not position" has its pluses and minuses. People like this definition because a management title does not a leader make. On the other hand, undisciplined or unfocused action can drive a company in circles or into the ground — and that's not what we want from leaders. So, again it fails the useful test.

Or consider, "a leader is someone you choose to follow to a place you wouldn't go by yourself." There's a positive aspect to this definition — we want inspiring leaders who are worth following. But, at the same time, we don't necessarily want to follow people to places we wouldn't go if we knew better — consider Jim Jones and his followers' mass suicide, Ken Lay and Enron's demise or all the executives who inspired followers into the dot-com bust or the financial meltdown.

> **Women Haven't Been Told...**
>
> That conventional wisdom about leadership leads them astray.

Some people define a leader saying what it is not — a manager. This definition doesn't work in all organizations — not all social movements have anointed managers. And, you'll read more later on about why this definition isn't useful.

I couldn't find a single definition that I felt comfortable with, so I set out to create one. Because of my 20 years practicing leadership and observing leadership in practice, I had developed a long view. And because I was refreshingly unencumbered by conventional wisdom, I could look at the concept of leadership with fresh eyes.

I began by identifying very specific criteria that my chosen definition would have to meet. It would have to be:

1. **Universal**. Apply to leaders around the globe, of all races, genders and nationalities.
2. **Ubiquitous**. Apply to leaders of all types of organizations: corporations, not-for-profits, social movements, governments, NGOs and religious institutions.
3. **Prescriptive**. Define what a leader *should* do, thereby ruling out people like Hitler or Osama bin Laden.

4. **Relevant to every level**. Conventional wisdom had long (and rightly) held that leadership can exist at any level from the individual contributor on the front line to the executive in the C-suite.
5. **Useful**. At the end of the day, someone would be able to use it to assess whether she had done a good job at leadership that day.

Next, I created a long list of people considered by many to be exemplars of leadership. Among the dozens of names on the list were:
○ Nelson Mandela, Desmond Tutu and Wangari Maathai from Africa.
○ From Asia, Mahatma Gandhi, Mother Teresa and Aung San Suu Kyi.
○ From the West, several U.S. presidents, Winston Churchill, General Patton, Queen Elizabeth, Joan of Arc, Elizabeth Cady Stanton, Sojourner Truth, Oprah Winfrey, Anne Mulcahy and Margaret Sanger.

Then I carefully studied this list for what it could teach me about leadership, and I learned three things:

First, to get on the list, each of the individuals had produced some outcome. They had created social change, built organizations, rescued failing organizations, empowered vast numbers to improve their lives, won wars, extended empires and more. Clearly, one element of leadership had to do with producing outcomes — in some way, changing the status quo.

Second, the exemplars of leadership behaved differently from other outcome-producers such as Hitler, Osama bin Laden and others like them. Both groups produced outcomes and had followers, but what they engaged in their followers was dramatically different. The exemplars engaged hope, optimism, egalitarianism, compassion, inclusion, passion, freedom, understanding, tolerance and the creative spirit. Hitler and others in his set engaged fear, hatred, bigotry, superiority; they used suppression and repression.

So to be prescriptive, another element of the definition had to touch on engaging the best in people.

Third, all of the exemplars drew on personal qualities that enabled them to lead effectively. For example, Eleanor Roosevelt's commitment to human rights and personal courage, Mahatma Gandhi's belief in the power of non-violence, Joan of Arc's fearlessness and faith, women's and civil rights advocate Sojourner Truth's resilience, Nobel Peace Prize winner Wangari Maathai's vision and more. No two of them were exactly alike, each drew on unique strengths, attributes and beliefs. So the third element of leadership has to do with using personal greatness.

A New — and Useful — Definition of Leadership

Based on this analysis, I came to understand that, simply stated,

> *Leadership is using the greatness in you to achieve and sustain extraordinary outcomes by engaging the greatness in others.*

This definition works because it is prescriptive (rules out Hitler), universal (applies to anyone, anywhere), ubiquitous (works for corporations and any other entity), relevant to any level (individual contributors to executives can find guidance in this definition) and it is useful (you can guide and evaluate your leadership behaviors with it).

In the model below, you can see the three interrelated elements of the definition. Each feeds and is fed by the other. Everything a leader does can be tied to these three components. No leader can execute the practice of leadership nor fulfill the promise of leadership without all three. This is another thing that women haven't been told about leadership.

I've been privileged to share this definition and model with many women (and men) who have used it to become increasingly effective leaders and to make progress in their careers. And that's what *No Ceiling, No Walls* is about — helping you to understand and use this definition as *your* foundation for continued career success.

The Missing 33%

Once I came to this definition, I discovered an unexpected and very welcome side benefit. Not only is the definition new to women, it also highlights another thing about leadership that women haven't been told. I call this the Missing 33%.

For years, you've probably heard a career success equation that touches on two of the three parts of my definition. It goes something like this:

Professional Competence + People Skills = Higher Leadership Positions

Professional competence is one aspect of "using the greatness in you." *People skills* are one element of "engaging the greatness in others."

You find the formula embedded in advice like this from coaching guru Marshall Goldsmith, "...*your people skills often make the difference in how high you go. Who would you rather have as a CFO? A moderately good accountant who is great with people...or a brilliant accountant who's inept with [people]...The candidate with superb people skills will win out every time, in large part because he will be able to...lead.*"

While the traditional formula touts "superb people skills" as the make-or-break element for career success, it's not the make-or-break element in the success formula for women. If it were, we'd already be represented in higher numbers at the top of organizations because study after study touts our superb people skills.

For us, the make-or-break element missing from this success equation is *business skills*. It's the assumed competence and is generally unspoken in discussions about leadership. But my definition of leadership brings it into the spotlight. It's the Missing 33%.

Assuming that professional competence also includes personal excellence, the true career success formula for women *and* men is this:

Professional Competence + People Skills + Business Skills = Higher Leadership Positions

We don't hear about it this way because, as mentioned earlier, the traditional success formula has been based on studies of men. Men are assumed to have a more natural inclination toward business skills and are more likely to be mentored or groomed for them. This explains why a recent DDI report found that at the first-line supervisor level 28% more men are in "high potential" programs, a variance that increases to 50% at the executive level!

Women Haven't Been Told...

About the importance of business skills to their success.

When it comes to leadership and career success, women haven't been told about the importance of business skills in leadership and achieving career goals. With its focus on achieving and sustaining outcomes, my definition of leadership, unlike others before it, puts as much emphasis on business skills (including business acumen, strategic acumen and financial acumen) as on the generally over-emphasized interpersonal skills. *No Ceiling, No Walls* will help you proudly present contrary evidence to the stereotype that women don't have business skills!

If you and I were sitting together in your office or in your living room, I would tell you that the most important professional contributions I've made in my life are my definition of leadership and my unconventional wisdom about the Missing 33%. Though I'm not seated with you, I offer them here and in subsequent chapters with the hope that you will use them to become the leader you seek to be, build the career you seek to have and live a meaningful and rewarding life.

You now have a definition of leadership that women haven't been told, and you've learned about the Missing 33% of the success formula for women. There are many other things that women haven't been told about leadership. And you'll be discovering them as you read along.

LESSONS IN LEADERSHIP

1. Leadership has three interdependent components:
   a. Using personal greatness,
   b. Achieving and sustaining extraordinary outcomes,
   c. Engaging the greatness in others.
2. Business skills (including business, strategic and financial acumen) are the Missing 33% in the career success equation for women.

Words Do Matter

"What's in a name? That which we call a rose
By any other name would smell as sweet."
—William Shakespeare

If, in the past, you've found the concept of leadership confusing, you're not alone. I know that for me, trying to grasp and hold onto what it means to be a leader was like trying to grab hold of air. One of the reasons the ideas of *leader* and *leadership* are so hard to nail down is that the terms are applied without discipline. Words do matter. And precise understanding and use of the word *leader* is essential to solidify an understanding of leadership.

Consider these three instances where careful use of the word *leader* are especially helpful. You should:

1. Not use *leader* as a synonym for executive.
2. Not use *leader* as a synonym for entrepreneur or inventor.
3. Not get caught in the dated concept of *leader* versus manager.

Leader is not a Synonym for Executive!

One of the reasons there's so much confusion about leadership is because the word *leader* is frequently used as a synonym for the CEO or a member of the executive team. This gives rise to confusion because it seems to indicate that if you aspire to be a leader, you simply have to reach a certain organizational level. That's clearly not true. Responsibility for (or authority over) people does not a leader make.

Here's why — based on our definition, not all people who produce outcomes deserve to be described as leaders (think of Hitler who improved the German economy), not all CEOs or executives deserve to be described as leaders (think of Ken Lay, former CEO of Enron) and, executives and senior managers who are not focused on achieving and sustaining outcomes by engaging the greatness in others, (as many of you know from personal experience).

I suggest that it is unwise and inaccurate to refer to such CEOs, executives or governmental heads in the same breath and with the same word *(leader)* as Mahatma Gandhi, who led the movement for India's independence from Great Britain, or Anne Mulcahy, who marshaled widespread employee commitment to rescue Xerox from the brink of bankruptcy.

Women Haven't Been Told…

That precise understanding and use of the word *leader* is essential to solidify an understanding of leadership.

So, instead of calling the group at the top of your organization the "leadership team," consider calling them the "executive team" — unless, of course, they all meet the definition.

Leader is not a Synonym for Entrepreneur or Inventor

During a discussion in one of my leadership programs, Joan said, *"I don't think people who sit in the CEO chair are leaders. The real leaders are those who invent something new."* She was right to express admiration for inventors, but her comment illustrates confusion about the differences between *leaders, entrepreneurs* and *inventors.*

Entrepreneur: someone who creates a business. The business may be built around the entrepreneur's invention or that of someone else. The entrepreneur may or may not meet our definition of leader, so an entrepreneur might or might not be a leader.

Inventor: someone who conceives of something new. An inventor may or may not create a business around his/her invention.

Leader: someone who meets our definition of using his/her personal greatness to achieve and sustain extraordinary outcomes by engaging the greatness in others.

Someone might be a great:
- Entrepreneur AND a great leader, but not an inventor.
- Inventor, but not an entrepreneur and not a business leader.
- Leader and be neither an inventor nor an entrepreneur.

Save the word *leader* for someone who meets our definition, and the words *entrepreneur* and *inventor* for people who create businesses or inventions.

Do *Leaders* Really Differ from *Managers?*

THEN *"**Managers** are people who do things right and **leaders** are people who do the right thing."*
Warren Bennis and Burt Nanus

NOW *"At every level, leadership means doing the right things **and** doing them right!"*
Susan L. Colantuono

The notion that managers are different from leaders is frequently represented as:

Leader	Manager
• Doing the *Right* Things	• Doing Things *Right*
• Leading Hearts and Minds	• Managing Results
• Transformational	• Transactional
• Who You Are	• What You Do

To understand how the idea of "leader versus manager" came into being and why it caught on, let me take you back in time because the idea arose from attempts in the late 1970s and early '80s to differentiate effective from ineffective executives.

This was a turbulent time for American business. The challenges of global competition from Japan and then Europe were raising questions about the viability of American businesses. Information technology was exploding from back-office processing to operational processing as the cost of automation rapidly declined. The Civil Rights movement was bringing increasing diversity into the workplace. Deregulation was boosting competition. Smokestack industries were failing.

In the face of these changes, some executives were successfully transforming their organizations — and reaping the profits. They were reading the external environment, setting strategic direction and engaging their workforce in change. Other executives were not. Instead, they were delivering business-as-usual and falling behind the market. In some cases, they didn't have the ability to read the business environment. In other cases, they had information about the business environment, but they made poor decisions. In many cases, they had as strongly loyal followers traveling down the mistaken path as the effective executives had loyal followers traveling the path of transformation.

In this turbulent time, researchers, practitioners and the business press focused attention on the effective executives. They recognized the very real difference between the great managers/executives who were transforming their companies and the inadequate managers/

executives who were maintaining the status quo and falling behind in the face of rapid and revolutionary change. Why did these differences in performance effectiveness become coded as the polarizing concept of *leader* versus *manager*?

At the time, there was no language for differentiating successful executives who were transforming organizations from those who weren't. Instead of differentiating *highly competent* from *less competent* executives, they called the effective executives *leaders*. But these executives were simply doing what they were being paid to do in a time of extraordinary change, i.e. read the environment, make intelligent decisions to keep growth, cash, return and customer in balance and engage people in change. Instead of identifying the ineffective executives as just that, they were called *managers*. They were singled out for *managing* when, in fact, they were failing in their executive responsibilities.

Many consultants, trainers, leadership researchers and boards of directors grabbed onto the sexy, celebrity-ripe notion of the visionary leader and off they went. They focused companies on generating powerful visions, helping "leaders" communicate these visions and searching for charismatic CEOs. They created vast bodies of research, management development programs, succession planning models and CEO selection parameters based on the premise that "manager" and "leader" are opposite ends of a continuum — with a distinct bias in favor of "leader."

And so the myth spread: you're EITHER a *manager* OR a *leader*.

I'm sure it's obvious to you that these terms aren't neutral. Because those being featured were successful executives, the attributes that the word *leader* represented was a success constellation. They were visionary, focused on the right things and transforming their organizations. Obviously, it was (and is) *better* to be a *leader*. This inherent bias has caused damage. For example, the main premise of Larry Bossidy and Ram Charan's excellent book, *Execution*, is that executives who had been disproportionately focused on vision need to refocus on execution (in other words, traditionally defined management) in order to deliver improved outcomes and shareholder value.

I thought this distinction between *manager* and *leader* indefensible when it emerged in the late 1970s and I still do. When I hear a woman say, "I want to be a leader, not a manager," I shake my head in dismay. Today, we face increasingly challenging environments, a flatter world, and more rapid proliferation of technology. We need people who can deliver on the whole package. People like Anne Mulcahy, former CEO, and Ursula Burns, CEO of Xerox. When they describe Xerox's remarkable turnaround, they give examples of:

- Focusing on cash and growth (doing the right things) *and* building basic business excellence and disciplined management of inventory (doing things right).
- Engaging employees' passion and talents (hearts and minds) *and* also their willingness to do anything to help Xerox succeed (efforts).
- Having a vision (transformation) *and* focusing on operational cash flow (results).
- Their personal strengths (who you are) *and* their personal actions (what you do).

Anne and Ursula demonstrate that the traditional, either/or model of *leader versus manager* is useless when studying great acts of business leadership. I hope it's clear how they illustrate that the paradigm of *manager versus leader* is a poor one on which to base your definition of leadership.

> **Women Haven't Been Told...**
> To distrust the idea of "leader *versus* manager"

Instead, understand that competent managers at all levels *must* drive change. Competent managers at all levels *must* lead. True leadership competence is not an either/or — it's a both/and, a yin and yang. Leadership competence means doing the right thing AND doing it right. It means managing others through capable processes AND engaging their hearts and minds. It means focusing on transactions AND on transformation. To be competent, whether you're an individual contributor, supervisor, manager or executive, you must be a leader who uses your personal greatness to achieve and sustain extraordinary outcomes by engaging the greatness in others. Effective executives and managers are leaders by definition. Those who don't meet our definition are ineffective.

From Here Forward

Words do matter. So, to help cement your understanding of leadership, throughout the rest of the book, here's how you'll see the following words used:

> *Leader:* someone who uses personal greatness to achieve and sustain extraordinary outcomes by engaging the greatness in others.

> *Executive:* someone who has responsibility for positioning the organization for success and authority over a team of senior managers and/or businesses. An executive may or may not meet the definition of a leader.

> *Manager:* someone who has responsibility for and authority over the work of multiple supervisors or teams. There are many levels of management (e.g. middle management, senior management). A manager may or may not meet the definition of a leader.

> *Supervisor:* someone who has responsibility for and authority over the work of a team of individual contributors. A supervisor may or may not meet the definition of a leader.

> *Individual Contributor:* someone who has no direct responsibility for or authority over the work of others. An individual contributor may or may not meet the definition of a leader.

I hope you'll adopt this as well. It will help you hold a crystal-clear understanding of leadership.

LESSONS IN LEADERSHIP

1. Reserve the word *leader* to describe those who use personal greatness to achieve and sustain extraordinary outcomes by engaging the greatness in others.
2. The idea that you're either a leader *or* a manager is a dated and a shaky basis for leadership development.
3. Precision in language will help you (and others) better understand leadership and develop as a leader. Refer to people by level unless they meet the definition of leadership. For example, executive, manager, supervisor, individual contributor.

Leadership is Gender Neutral…
Perceptions are Not

*"The Pew Research Center, which examines attitudes
toward public policy issues, showed in an August study that
69 percent of American men and 68 percent of American
women think both genders make equally good leaders."*

The definition of leadership that we are working with is gender neutral. If you reflect on the faces of the men and women who are frequently named as good examples of leaders, it is obvious that leadership also transcends race, nationality, religion and physical ability. As additional evidence, we can look at the increasing numbers of women who have made it through corporate America to seats in the C-suite; women like Indra Nooyi of PepsiCo, Anne Mulcahy, former CEO of Xerox; Brenda Barnes, CEO of Sara Lee; Angela Braly, CEO of WellPoint; and Carly Fiorina of H-P. Each is evidence of the fact that the *practice* of leadership is neutral and that women and men are equally capable of standing at the helm of major corporations.

As a matter of fact, many studies point to the fact that women's inherent strengths set us firmly on the path to leadership. A *Business Week* cover story proclaimed "As Leaders, Women Rule." The article summarized several years' worth of studies in which women outperformed men on 50% to 85% of the skills measured by traditional assessments and performance reviews. The article explained,

> *"By and large the studies show that women executives, when rated by their peers, direct reports and bosses, score higher than their male counterparts on a wide variety of measures — from producing high-quality work to goal-setting to mentoring employees. Using elaborate performance evaluations of execs, researchers found that women got higher ratings than men on almost every skill measured."*

And, in the years since, new studies that reinforce these findings have been released. In the Fall of 2008, a survey conducted by the White House Project, a women's leadership advocacy group, reported that women outranked or tied men in four of five leadership qualities — honesty, intelligence, compassion and creativity. (Men trumped women on decisiveness.) Another recent study of 65,000 found that women make good leadership material because we are viewed as innately altruistic, people-oriented, co-operative and open.

The reports of our successes and leadership attributes might be cause for celebration for women around the country, but for me, they are disturbing. I ask, if we're so good, why are there so few of us at the top? Today's amazing C-suite women remain the exception, not the rule. As of 2008, the percentage of women in F500 corporate officer positions was a mere 15.7%, down from 16.4% in 2005. In the U.S., the top 25 highest-paid men made $1.3 billion, 4.35 times more than the top 25 best-paid women. And no woman cracked the ranks of top 25 highest-paid executives overall.

I found a clue about why there are so few of us at the top in the subtitle of the *Business Week* article. It read, *"New studies find that female managers outshine their male counterparts in almost every measure."* Ah ha! *Almost* every measure. I realized that the measures on which male managers outperformed women would be of profound significance. So I searched for those items to compare them with the areas where women outperformed men, and here is what I discovered.

Women are seen by bosses as outperforming men in the areas of interpersonal skills, including sensitivity to others, willingness to listen, ability to work with diverse people, developing people, getting results through people, forming close relationships with others and giving feedback. We are seen as good at following through using project management-type skills and tools; and as pushing for results, achievement-oriented and having high expectations of others. If we put these results in the context of the definition of leadership, in study after study women are viewed as being effective at *"engaging the greatness in others"* and at exhibiting professional skills *(using personal greatness)*.

On the other hand, men are viewed by bosses as outperforming women in the areas of business acumen, which includes having "business smarts" (an instinct for making money and exploiting business opportunities) and understanding financial issues. They are also viewed as outperforming women in the area of strategic acumen, including innovation, taking a long-range view to problem solving, seeing the big picture, effective decisions and being comfortable in a fast-change environment. In other words, when it comes to the *"achieving and sustaining outcomes"* part of our leadership definition, men win hands down.

And, finally, men are viewed as more skilled in strategic relationships, winning others to their point of view and using organizational resources (defined as: able to build alliances, sophisticated about organizational dynamics, having many contacts and delegating with autonomy). So while women are seen as having better interpersonal skills overall, men are seen as better at employing relationships in service of goals — "aligning others." In a way, research by Catalyst describes these advantages when they report that women continue to be expected to "take care" while men are expected to "take charge."

Men's perceived strengths can be summed up as business acumen, strategic acumen, delegation, strategic relationships, financial acumen and creating a vision. These are the "corner office" skills that

Deborah Merrill Sands, Co-Director of Simmons Center on Gender and Organization, refers to when she says, *"Companies may say they want collaborative leaders, but they still hold deep-seated beliefs that top managers need to be heroic figures. Interpersonal skills may be recognized as important, but they aren't explicitly seen as corner-office skills."* The corner-office skills — such as business acumen, strategic acumen and financial acumen — are under-represented in many management training and leadership development programs. These are the skills where, in study after study, women are perceived as underperforming in relation to men. And these are the very skills that women have to develop, hone and demonstrate. These are the Missing 33% in the leadership success formula.

The disappointing statistics and research results tell us that, while the *practice* of leadership is gender neutral, the *perception* of women as leaders and potential leaders is NOT.

Leadership Development Challenges

> **Women Haven't Been Told...**
>
> That traditional leadership development programs aren't equally effective for men and women.

So how good are organizations at dealing with these unequal perceptions? Well, they could be better. Many rely on their leadership development programs to put women and men on equal footing — and have been doing so since the 1970s. But their frameworks are often based on studies of successful male executives who were noted for their interpersonal skills because they were required to engage followers in organizational transformation. As a result, most management/leadership training programs over-emphasize the development of interpersonal skills and personal greatness and under-emphasize or totally omit business acumen skills.

Let me illustrate. Consider these two lists of topics offered in management or leadership workshops. Which are offered in your company?

Coaching Others	Business Acumen
Motivating Staff	Leveraging Strategic Relationships
Developing Others	Financial Acumen
Managing Conflict	Strategy Formulation
Team Building	Strategy Execution
Giving Feedback	Leading for Outcomes
Facilitating Meetings	Leader as Process Owner
Managing Change	
Dealing with Difficult People	
Communication Skills	
Active Listening	
Dialogue	
Negotiation Skills	

Chances are you recognize more topics on the left than on the right. Companies have been offering courses like those on the left for years. Are they important? Yes. Do they help women confront the biased perception of their capability as leaders? No.

These programs hone the interpersonal skills that women are noted for (and men are not) and many excel at. They give short shrift to the "corner office" skills that women are perceived as lacking. As long as conventional wisdom and corporate leadership development programs focus on engaging others and personal excellence, women will be underserved. Instead, they have to identify the full complement of skills required to practice leadership and provide programming and experiences that fill gaps women have in the areas of business, strategic and financial acumen and strategic networking. And we have to manage our careers to fill those gaps as well.

Irene Rosenfeld, CEO of Kraft, did just that. She used a stint at General Foods to hone her strategic understanding of and focus on growth through innovation. John Bowlin, her boss at General Foods, praised her business savvy saying, "She really understands the consumer. She has the innate ability to translate that into an appropriate *business strategy*."

Organizations could do a better job dealing with unequal perceptions in another way. They could move away from subjective appraisals of potential (often competency-based) and do a better job of assessing leadership potential on quantitative measures.

It's no accident that *Fortune* magazine found that companies with the highest concentration of women at the top are "fanatical" about measurement...they use *"empirical standards, clear goals and frequent reviews to identify and reward high performers."* By downplaying subjective *perceptions* of competence and focusing on the achievement of outcomes, women in these companies get beyond the biased perceptions of leadership potential and are able to excel in the neutral practice of leadership.

Isn't leadership neutral? Absolutely, but as we've seen, the *perception* of women and men as leaders is biased. Organizations continue to suffer from these unequal *perceptions*...and in that way, continue to suffer from an inability to ensure that the best-qualified people get to the top. Organizations continue to offer leadership training programs that fill the perceived gaps in men's leadership competencies, leaving you on your own to figure out how to acquire, develop and demonstrate the skills that will power your career success.

Armed with the knowledge that the perceptions of women as leaders are not neutral, you can pick and choose the skills you need to acquire, develop or showcase in order to achieve your career goals.

LESSONS IN LEADERSHIP

1. The *practice* of leadership is absolutely gender neutral.
2. The *perception* of women and men as leaders is not neutral. In the context of our definition of leadership,
   a. Women are seen as better at engaging others and at personal greatness.
   b. Men are seen as better at leading for outcomes.
3. Leading for outcomes trumps interpersonal skills on the path to the corner office.
4. If these generalizations apply to you, it's important for you to have learning experiences (in courses and on-the-job) that allow you to hone your ability to lead for outcomes.

Anyone at Any Level Can Wear the Mantle of Leadership

"Only when we know what we're made of and what we want to make of it can we begin our lives…people begin to become leaders at that moment when they decide for themselves how to be."

—WARREN BENNIS

Traditionally, when a queen is crowned, she dons the mantle and takes the staff of royalty. These are symbols of elevated responsibility. You're lucky. You don't have to wait to have someone give you your mantle of leadership. You can don it yourself. And when you do, the path to advancement gets a little clearer.

Beyond a certain point, career progression (promotion) isn't about getting "grades" for individual work or recognition for good behavior. While you might be able to work at a job for a lifetime, you can only advance if you're willing to don the mantle of leadership. This is something that John (not his real name) knew.

After attending one of my workshops on strategic acumen — where, I'm sad to report, 85% of the attendees were men — John approached to thank me for the program. During our conversation, he said, *"I want to be a great leader."* Now, John isn't an MBA who would reasonably be expected to have this insight. He was a Ph.D. biophysicist who realized that, after a certain point, success wouldn't be about doing his science. It would be all about leadership. He's not the only man who understands this. Legendary repeat-success CEO James McNerney says, "I have this idea in mind — all of us get 15 percent better every year. Usually [this] means our **ability to lead**...."

Do you want to be a great leader? Instead of thinking that you are an individual to whom the company owes something, realize that you owe the company every contribution you can make to its success in the marketplace. Break free of thinking that you're acting for individual achievement, break out of self-limiting ideas and break through to a new understanding that you have a positional purpose — to lead others in support of the organization's goals. And you can do this no matter your level!

When I had the honor of working with Jane Metzger, then Chief Nursing Officer of Rhode Island Hospital, as she launched shared governance at the hospital, we educated the nurses who became members of shared governance councils. Among other things they learned how to be leaders at the bedside and with their colleagues. Using my definition of leadership, we conducted a yearly meeting that was an orientation of new council members and a refresher for existing members.

During each year's orientation meeting, we asked the nurses to brainstorm a list of people they thought were exemplars of leaders. The first year, the answers were predictably similar to those I listed in Chapter 1. The next year, Lori, a staff nurse from Hasbro Children's Hospital, stood up and said, *"I am a leader."* Jane and I were thrilled. Lori had taken on the mantle of leadership. And, as a result, her career has blossomed.

Being for the Business

Wearing the mantle of leadership in business means that you understand and act on the fact that you are *for the company and by extension for the customer.* It means being for the business. Merrill Sherman, CEO of Bank Rhode Island, describes that as one of the most valuable pieces of advice she received early in her career — *"be for the company."* Ursula Burns, CEO of Xerox, offers similar advice when she says, *"Do everything you can to embrace opportunity, work hard, deliver results and make sure* **you focus on the firm first.**" And Ann Livermore, EVP of Hewlett Packard, also gave life to this idea. Hewlett Packard's acquisition of EDS and subsequent reorganization reduced Ann's technology solutions group by 13%. When asked about the decrease in staff, she responded, **"This isn't about me. It's about what is best for H-P.** *It makes sense to combine all outsourcing businesses — and with a merger this big, for EDS to report directly to [the CEO]."*

Susan Arnold, president of global business units for Proctor & Gamble, makes the same point when Patricia Sellers of *Fortune* asked her how she identifies people with extraordinary talent. Susan said, *"They're owners. They* **treat the business like they own it.** *They're lead-ers. They create a vision and lead people in that direction. They consistently deliver above expectations. They deliver. They deliver. They deliver. They create great organizations that can deliver without them."*

I hope you take two pieces of advice from Susan's comment. First, she is telling you that to succeed, you have to act like a business owner instead of think-ing that the business is there to take care of you. The second piece of advice in Susan's comment is that promotions aren't rewards for personal performance, they're earned on the basis of creating, achieving and sustaining outcomes! So, please don't look for the secret "five steps" or "seven tools" that if performed flawlessly will move you ahead. Don't believe that if your staff likes you, you've earned advancement. Don't believe if you "do the job," you'll get recognized. To succeed, you have to make the shift from doing the job through your competence to hitting organizational outcomes by leading others — in other words, by donning the mantle of leadership.

> **Women Haven't Been Told…**
>
> That wearing the mantle of leadership means acting like a business owner rather than an employee.

Wearing the mantle also means being positive. Instead of seeing problems and giving them power as you follow them down a vicious spiral of negativity, acknowledge problems and ride over them on the wheels of potential solutions. As Denise Nemchev, Staff Executive of Complex Management for Stanley Works, says, *"Solve problems, don't create them."*

Lynn Elsenhans, CEO of Sunoco, says this of her personal lessons as an executive, but it applies equally to anyone at any level: *"…a leader has to be more positive than negative and have a vision for the future and a belief that things can be better. People need a reason to believe and hope, and they will not follow a leader who doesn't have the view that tomorrow will be better than today."*

A slightly different take on being positive is Meg Whitman's. Meg is the former CEO of eBay who has said that throughout her career she wanted to be fun to work with and easy to manage *"because… when you have two people of equal competence and you have somebody who's easy to manage — you'll pick them every day of the week over the hard-to-manage person."*

Leaders @ Every Level™

You can don the mantle of leadership no matter the level you're at because leaders can and do exist at every level of any organization. Let me introduce Helen as an example of why I say this.

I first met Helen when I was consulting on a project to implement a new resource management system for the cancer program at an academic medical center. The implementation team included the vice president (as sponsor), two directors, two managers, an IS project manager and three administrative staff.

As the first meeting starts, I explain, "The first thing we're going to do is to map the big categories of work and who does them so we can get an idea of how the work flows." Minutes after we begin, Helen raises her voice and says, "We have too many open billing codes."

Having never worked in a medical clinic, I have no idea what she means. "Does that have anything to do with the process we're mapping?" I ask. She answers, "No." I ask if it's okay to put the issue on the parking lot for later discussion and we return to mapping the process.

At the next meeting, we drill down to map the process in further detail and Helen again says, "We have too many open billing codes."

"Thanks, Helen," I say, "that's on the parking lot and we'll get to it when we finish this part of the project." We continue to map the process.

At the third meeting, once again, Helen raises her voice and says, "We have too many open billing codes." Okay, it's taken three efforts on her part, but I finally get it. I ask, "What is an open billing code and why does it matter if there are too many?"

With great patience, Helen says, "An open billing code is a procedure or medication we don't get paid for."

I am stunned. I ask, "How many open billing codes does the clinic have?" She proceeds to explain that about half of the billing codes are open and that she's been trying to rectify this problem by bringing it to people's attention for seven years!

I tell you this story because Helen wasn't the vice president on the team. She wasn't a director or manager or supervisor; she was an administrative professional. Helen is a tremendous example of leadership at the individual contributor level. Why? Let's use our definition of leadership to analyze her actions:

Use the greatness in you: It is apparent that Helen drew on business acumen, analytical ability, courage and personal resilience to persist for seven years in trying to rectify the problem and to achieve a positive outcome for the clinic.

Achieve and sustain extraordinary outcomes: Helen was focused (more than her manager or perhaps even the vice president) on the profitability of the clinic. She understood the relationship between the billing codes and revenue.

Engage the greatness in others: Helen knew the right people to enlist to solve this problem (it wasn't her fault that they did not act) and she seized yet another opportunity to engage me as an outsider whose project had nothing to do with revenue generation.

Wondering what happened? Here's the end of the story. Helen and I worked with others in the hospital to reduce the number of open billing codes. In the first **month** following the fix, an additional $250,000 of revenue came into the clinic. Imagine the revenue if the problem had been corrected when Helen first raised it seven years before.

Peter Drucker once said, *"The most important element for today's organizations is leadership — the highest in demand and lowest in supply."* I tell Helen's story because I think Drucker's point is inaccurate. There's plenty of leadership in supply today, but Helen teaches us that we have to know what to look for, where to find it and how to cultivate it. If you're a supervisor, manager or executive looking for high potential talent, Helen's a leadership mentor because she teaches that the definition of leadership can help you recognize leadership at any level. By looking for employees at any level who use personal greatness to deliver outcomes by engaging other people, you are on track for identifying emerging leaders.

Conventional wisdom has long held that leadership exists at and should be drawn from every level of the organization. Helen is living proof of this. She teaches us that you can demonstrate leadership long before being promoted to a supervisory position. You begin to develop and demonstrate leadership at the individual contributor level. Here are some of the ways that you can don the mantle of leadership and act like a business owner no matter your level:

- If you see a problem, don't complain; take action with others to get it fixed.
- Treat your organization as if you own it. Lead for outcomes in a way that engages others and brings out the best in them. If you create a team that can deliver without you, you are free to move on to the next challenge.
- Speak positively about your organization in public.

- Think of yourself as a leader and always behave as if others are watching you (which, by the way, they are).

LESSONS IN LEADERSHIP

1. Donning the mantle of leadership means:
   a. Being for the business (acting like you own it).
   b. Seeing where the organization is going and leading others there.
   c. Delivering, delivering, delivering.
2. There are leaders at every level.
3. The higher you go, the more your success depends not on your individual competence but on how well you wear the mantle of leadership.
4. It's never too early to begin to demonstrate leadership. Use the definition of leadership to find ways to lead from wherever you are.
5. It's never too early to begin to cultivate leadership in others. Use the definition to look for emerging leaders and help them develop their leadership skills.

Leadership Differs by Level

"A whole new learning curve faced me: how to be chief executive officer of a public company with obligations to shareholders, how to apply what little I'd learned about management to the business of the company. ...I didn't know how and when to think about growth, how the job description of a chief executive office would read, how much profit we should be making or should be aiming to make."
—KATHARINE GRAHAM, FORMER CHAIRMAN AND CEO
WASHINGTON POST COMPANY
PERSONAL HISTORY

You might be wondering, does leadership differ by level? Does leadership look different at the executive level as compared to middle management? The answer is yes, leadership differs by level. Though leadership can be demonstrated at the individual contributor level, it looks different at the supervisor level. Though you can master leadership as a supervisor, you will have to learn different skills to lead as a manager. And, as Katharine Graham's quote illustrates, what she learned prior to moving to the CEO's position wouldn't suffice now that she was at the top.

As you move up the organization, leadership skills are additive — at each higher level you will have to take on the new leadership responsibilities of that level. And the obsessions are subtractive. At each higher level, you will have to shed some of the non-essential skills, responsibilities and actions you mastered while in the job you left. Sticking with those comfortable skills and actions can be a career-derailing obsession.

Helen Greiner, chairman and co-founder of iRobot, is an example of an executive who understood the additive and subtractive nature of advancement. To free herself up to cultivate relationships with venture capitalists and pitch for capital (her job as the CEO), she gave up scientific work she loved doing and hired a research director. Her understanding that leadership differs by level helped her make the transition from tech geek to effective executive.

Let's explore what this means across all levels.

Individual Contributor

When you're at career-start as an individual contributor, you demonstrate mastery by knowing your job inside and out and by meeting your individual goals. Like Helen of the open billing codes story, some of the ways you can demonstrate leadership include:

- Being a role model for high performance. (Use Personal Greatness)
- Recognizing and making suggestions for improvements. (Achieve Outcomes)
- Teaming with others to meet or exceed goals. (Engage Others)

Moving Up to Supervisor/Team Lead

As a supervisor or project/team lead, you still need your individual contributor skills, but you are being paid to shift your focus from meeting goals through your individual performance to leading a group of individual contributors for *team success*. This requires that you demonstrate leadership by adding the ability to:

- Understand how your team contributes to organizational success. (Use Personal Greatness)
- Create a high-performing team. (Achieve Outcomes)
- Create a high-retention culture. (Engage Others)

This also means that you have to let go. You let go of the obsession of performing the individual contributor work that you were skilled at — work that's now the responsibility of your direct reports — so you have time to nurture, develop and align your team.

Mastering the Middle

When you're promoted to a management position, you're paid to lead multiple teams for a visible impact on organizational outcomes. You draw on all you've learned as an individual contributor and supervisor and take those leadership skills with you. The added leadership skills you cultivate include:

- Professional Vision — the passion about your profession and the organization to relentlessly pursue innovation; to stay current at what's happening in your profession or industry and to look for other trends or innovations that could impact your organization. (Use Personal Greatness)
- A deep understanding of the business of business — what's valuable to the customer, how all the parts of the organization work together to deliver value to the customer and where in the value chain are your teams. To expand her business understanding, Liz Smith, president of Avon, left a position running Kraft Food's major Jell-O division to work in a small U.S. import business. There she gained experience in sales and global distribution. (Achieve Outcomes)
- Peripheral Vision — the ability to look outside your division/department and recognize opportunities to collaborate with other managers to improve processes for improved outcomes. When Carrie Cox was EVP and president of global pharmaceuticals for Schering-Plough, she made a similar point, *"The sooner you create that peripheral vision and global mindset, the faster you can excel."* (Engage Others)

As a manager, you let go of the obsession of directly supervising individual contributors within your span of control. Instead, you reach them indirectly by coaching your direct reports (supervisors and managers). You also let go of your singular focus on day-to-day operations and begin to think strategically.

The View from the Top

All of the preceding leadership skills come with you but are insufficient when you are promoted to an executive position. Now you are paid to position the organization for success. Andrea Jung, CEO of Avon Products, Inc., makes this point in a *Wall Street Journal* (WSJ) interview, *"The skills that landed me the job [of CEO], that I thought would carry more weight today, are still there. But I've had to learn and grow and **develop tremendously different skills sets in the corner office.**"*

What are those different skills required at the executive level? They are to:

- Hone skills needed for rigorous and productive external relationships. (Use Personal Greatness)
- Understand broad external trends (e.g. demographic, industry, societal), analyze the impact on the company and set strategy. (Achieve Outcomes)
- Maintain resolve and focus for the organization. (Achieve Outcomes)
- Ensure development, execution and ongoing adjustment of strategy. As described by Bev Behan, founder of Board Advisor, LLC, *"Creates and articulates a future shared vision for the company based on the financial, political and technical aspects of the business and industry."* (Achieve Outcomes)
- Network outside the organization with customers, shareholders, legislators, donors, peers, suppliers, alliance partners and others who can contribute to organizational success. Or, from this example of CEO selection criteria described by Bev, *"Seeks out opportunities to represent the company and its leadership in order to develop positive relationships with external and internal constituency groups."* (Engage Others)

- Interact with the board and set conditions for board effectiveness. (Engage Others)

To illustrate the view from the top, here's a summary job requirement for a CFO position. What do you notice about it?

"The CFO can take responsibility for or assist with fundraising efforts, negotiate contracts, develop relationships with bankers, attorneys, insurance agents and other third parties; develop and update forecasts and create or be a key member of the team creating the strategic business plan."

I hope you see that leadership at the executive level includes external relationships, trend analysis and strategy creation. All help position the organization in its external environment.

Another example is provided by Kathleen Hittner, M.D., CEO of The Miriam Hospital and chair of the Rhode Island Airport Authority. Kathleen spoke about her view from the top of The Miriam Hospital as part of a leadership program I facilitated. Commenting that the hospital and airport authority were very different organizations, one of the participants asked her how she did both jobs. Kathleen replied, *"At my level, the two jobs are very much the same. The Miriam had to grow and the airport has to grow. For both, growth plans generated community opposition. For both, we had to make a decision to move forward. For both, we had to work with the community."*

Her executive perspective is clear. She is focused on positioning both organizations for future success. She is focused on external forces and external relationships. She is clear that both organizations had to proceed with resolve and that she is the voice of resolve for the organizations.

At the executive level, what do you let go of? Among the most important is to let go of the impulse to personally make operational decisions — instead, you rely on your senior managers to do that with your guidance and/or coaching.

Board Level

In the first half of 2009, more women had been appointed to corporate boards than ever before. I find this a heartening statistic and hope you do, too, because several studies point to a correlation between the percentages of women on boards and both company performance and the strength of the internal pipeline for women. If you aspire to hold a director position, you might be wondering what does leadership look like at the board level?

Individual directors may hold positions of leadership as committee chairs or board chairs, but to be effective, they must also lead as individual contributors. So leadership at this level includes leading from a position of authority and from a position of membership. As guardians of the health and future viability of the organization, directors:

- Draw on the personal strengths and positive attributes they've developed over the years as a foundation for acquiring skills and knowledge that will make them effective board members. (Use Personal Greatness)
- Ensure that there is a strategy in place that fully addresses competitive threats and opportunities. (Achieve Outcomes)
- Assess the state of the business. They read the financials for the story they tell about the organization's alignment with (or lack of alignment with) the strategy and ensure appropriate actions are taken. (Achieve Outcomes)
- Ensure that there is an enterprise risk assessment/crisis management plan in place to protect the organization against foreseeable risk. (Achieve Outcomes)
- Monitor overall board performance and the individual performance of board members. (Achieve Outcomes and Engage Others)
- Assess CEO performance against financial goals and strategic outcome measures. (Engage Others)
- Act as a sounding board for the CEO and senior management on critical ideas and strategies. (Engage Others)
- Ensure appropriate plans are in place for CEO succession and execute the plans if necessary. (Engage Others)

- Replenish board membership — often selecting new members through their personal contacts with individuals or board search firms. (Engage Others)

> **Women Haven't Been Told...**
>
> That to move up the organization, they must understand how leadership differs by level.

What do directors let go of? Because they often are (or have been) executives and CEOs, they let go of their drive to make executive decisions. Bev Behan calls directors who can't drop their executive mindset, "CEO Wannabes." These are board members who are "constantly second-guessing the CEO" or chronically micromanaging.

What You See Depends on Where You Stand

This understanding of how leadership differs by level is useful when being promoted or when going after a promotion. What is a promotion? If you're like most people, you think of it first as a reward for past performance. But in reality, a promotion is a demand for future performance. You are promoted because someone sees evidence that you can perform at the next higher level of leadership.

When you are interested in or receive a promotion, you can use this understanding of how leadership differs by level to your advantage. The job you're applying for looks different to the hiring manager — who's looking down at it — than it does to you as you look up at it.

Let's say you report to Chris, Chris reports to Sam and you want Chris' job. Having worked for Chris for a while, you have an idea of the job that Chris does. On the other hand, you probably don't know everything that Sam expects of Chris. This means that to position yourself for a promotion to Chris' job, you have to first figure out how to view Chris' job through Sam's eyes and learn what successful performance means to Sam. How? A mentor or someone in your network at Sam's level can help. You then ask yourself what evidence you can provide to Sam (someone at least two levels above you) so that you can deliver what's needed in Chris' job (that's at least one level above you).

For example, if you're a supervisor and Chris is a manager — how can you demonstrate to a senior manager (Sam) your ability to build cohesion across teams or import innovation? If you're a manager and Chris is a director, Sam doesn't expect you to simply manage a larger scope. You'll be expected to help strategically position the organization. To have a shot at the promotion, you will want to demonstrate either the ability or capacity to recommend strategic initiatives.

When you understand how leadership differs by level, you can intentionally develop the skills you need to succeed from career-start to the C-suite and onto corporate boards. You might seek out a special project or temporary assignment or you could stretch beyond your role in the position you hold. Understanding how leadership differs by level also enables you to successfully navigate the transitions that come with each promotion — zeroing in on the skills you have to add and attending to what you have to stop doing. This is particularly important because a recent report by DDI reports that women are less likely to receive help in making these transitions than their male counterparts. Regardless of the level you are, the earlier you acquire the strategic perspective of successful executives, the greater your chances are of being seen as capable of moving up.

LESSONS IN LEADERSHIP

1. Leadership manifests at every level, but in different ways.
2. Leadership skills are additive as you move up the organization.
3. To be effective, you also have to stop activities as you move up.
4. The leadership responsibilities of jobs above you look different to the people in them and above them than they do to you.

You *Can* Learn to Lead

> *"If we cannot choose our circumstances, we can always choose our response to them. If we cannot choose who we are, we can always choose to become something more. To stop choosing is to start dying."*
> —CARLY FIORINA
> TOUGH CHOICES

In America, there's been a long-standing debate about whether people are born leaders or can learn to lead. For example, you might have heard, "leaders are born and not made" or "leaders can be developed." I'm going to put the debate to rest. Both are true. Some people have a natural skill set for leadership; others acquire it.

Leadership is comprised of a set of skills and knowledge that you can develop through disciplined practice. In his *Fortune* magazine article on excellence, Geoffrey Colvin writes, *"The most successful people need around 10 years of hard work before becoming world class, a pattern so well established researchers call it the 10-year rule."* Notice, he doesn't say 10 years holding a job or 10 years in a position. He is explicit; it takes 10 years of "hard work."

What the "hard work" of disciplined practice means for you is that once you've identified a

> **Women Haven't Been Told...**
> To use the skill of disciplined practice in order to learn and improve leadership skills.

41

leadership skill you want to improve, you have to approach it with three requirements:

1. Intention of bringing your performance beyond your current level,
2. Discipline to seek, receive and analyze feedback on your results, and
3. Opportunity for repetition in order to gauge improvement.

Disciplined practice is the hallmark of those who become great. Based on his definition of disciplined practice, Geoffrey Colvin writes, *"Anything that anyone does at work, from the most basic task to the most exalted, is an improvable skill."* This includes leadership.

You've already met Helen Greiner, chairman and co-founder of iRobot. To become the legendary technology executive she is today, Helen had to conquer her fear of public speaking. Before making a pitch, she would practice it over and over. And it's a good thing she did. In addition to highly experienced military audiences, Helen pitched to major venture capitalists around the world. She would never have landed the first $1.5 million investment if she hadn't used disciplined practice to transform from little skill (and much fear) to accomplished presenter. As a result of her disciplined practice, and since the iRobot IPO in 2005, Helen has raised an additional $38 million and the company hit $250 million in revenue in 2008.

Helen demonstrates that leadership skills are learnable, but not if you routinely slog through the day-to-day tasks of leadership. You have to approach each act of leadership with the goal of getting better at it. And there are many daily acts of leadership that lend themselves to improvement through disciplined practice. For example:

- *Using personal greatness* requires speaking with an authentic voice, using the power of language and leading in alignment with your espoused values — each an improvable skill.
- *Achieving and sustaining outcomes* involves analyzing your work for the key goals you support, understanding them in the context of organizational strategy, deciphering the business story behind financial numbers and making

decisions to drive key outcomes — each an improvable skill if you intentionally seek to improve, receive feedback on your results and repeat the cycle again the next time with a new performance goal.

- *Engaging the greatness in others* requires a host of communication skills, from active listening to managing meetings to strategic communication to cultivating and nurturing external strategic relationships — each an improvable skill.

That leadership is an improvable set of skills is not only supported by research on those who excel, but also by research into the malleability of the brain. One such body of research is that of Stanford's Carol Dweck, author of *Mindset: The Psychology of Success*.

Dweck differentiates two mindsets: the *fixed* and the *growth* mindsets. People holding a fixed mindset believe that intelligence is static and are likely to avoid challenges, feel threatened by negative feedback and exert little effort. Confront your *fixed* mindset when it rears its constraining head.

People holding a growth mindset believe that intelligence can be developed. They are likely to test themselves more, seek and accept feedback and view hard work as a path to mastery, not as a sign of lack of intelligence. This is the mindset of disciplined practice.

Susan Desmond-Hellman, Genentech's chief of product development, reflects a growth mindset when she says this about her career transition from physician to businesswoman, *"Do something you're passionate about and that challenges you. Ask yourself 'What will I learn from this?'* **Every day I learn something new** *at Genentech, and even though I didn't have a very well laid out career path, I think **I've learned and benefited from everything I did**."*

Dweck also studied whether one's mindset can be changed. The answer is yes. As so much of neuroscience is telling us, the brain is remarkably malleable! So, if you've been holding the fixed mindset idea that leaders are born and not made, read Dweck's book. Shift your mindset so that being armed with the knowledge that disciplined practice can help you develop as a leader, you can master the art of leadership.

Can you learn to lead? I hope I've convinced you that you can... if you tap your growth mindset and use disciplined practice on the skills you want to improve.

LESSONS IN LEADERSHIP

1. Leadership is comprised of a set of skills and knowledge that you can develop through disciplined practice.
2. You approach activities with either a *fixed* or *growth* mindset (which one we use can vary, depending on the activity). You can shift from a *fixed* to a *growth* mindset.
3. The *growth* mindset is the basis for improving your ability to lead.

The Three Elements of Leadership

Leadership is simple. Its simplicity lies in understanding that leadership means using the greatness in you to achieve and sustain extraordinary outcomes by engaging the greatness in others. But leadership is not easy. There's a lot to know and be able to do in order to be a great leader.

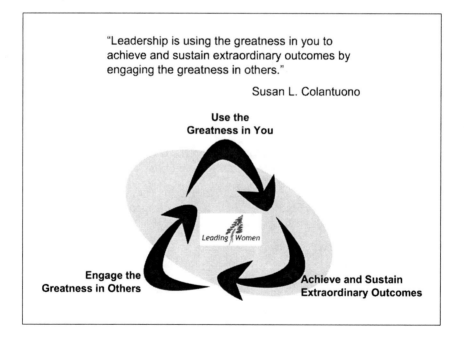

At the end of Part One, we affirmed that you *can* learn to lead. In Part Two, you'll discover the knowledge and skills you have to learn to counter the stereotypical perceptions of women as leaders.

Leadership Element	You'll learn to:
Achieve Extraordinary Outcomes	Understand and execute your positional purpose — your responsibility to hit outcomes in the areas of cash, growth, return and customer. This understanding rests on business, financial and strategic acumen.
Engage the Greatness in Others	Harness the power of strategic relationships by capturing the hearts, minds and efforts of people within and outside your organization and aligning them toward key outcomes.
Use Personal Greatness	Bring your authentic self, lead from your personal greatness and enhance your leadership presence.

You might be wondering what Part Two would cover if it were written solely for men and addressed the areas where men are seen as underperforming women or as lacking in leadership ability. I call these the 3 Es. With a touch of tongue in cheek and a rogues' gallery of failed CEOs in mind, here's what men need to learn.

Leadership Element	Men Need...
Achieve Extraordinary Outcomes	Ethics: to achieve outcomes in ways that are within the letter and the spirit of the law.
Engage the Greatness in Others	Emotional Intelligence: to engage and empower others with empathy, understanding and respect.
Use Personal Greatness	Egolessness: to put the organization ahead of personal ambition and give credit to others.

This part of the book is built around the three components of the definition of leadership:

Achieve and Sustain Extraordinary Outcomes
Lead for Outcomes
Think Like a CEO: Business Acumen
Chart a Course: Strategic Acumen
Show Me the Money: Financial Acumen
Use the Language of Power

Engage the Greatness in Others
Capture Hearts, Minds and Efforts
Develop Your 5-C Engagement Strategies
Align Others
Build Strategic Relationships

Use Personal Greatness
Lead from Personal Greatness, Part 1
Lead from Personal Greatness, Part 2
Mine the Power of Language
Tap the Power of Non-Verbals

At the end of each chapter, the **Lead ON!** section offers inspiring and practical actions, ready-to-apply tools and insights from self-assessments designed to help you enhance your leadership skills.

Focus Your Learning

It's likely that some of the chapters will be more important to you than others. You can use this mini-assessment to focus your learning.

Put yourself into your boss' shoes (or better yet, his/her boss' shoes) and rate yourself as you think your boss (or boss' boss) would rate you. Use this scale:

    1 = I don't see her demonstrate this at all.
    3 = I see occasional evidence of this.
    5 = She demonstrates potential in this area.
    7 = She fairly consistently demonstrates this.
  10 = She's a role model in this area.

1. _1_ Through her decisions, focus and language, she demonstrates deep knowledge of the business of our business.
2. _2_ She demonstrates and teaches others basic financial acumen.
3. _5_ She thinks strategically, understands strategic forces and sets strategy.
4. _1_ She uses a range of approaches to engage her colleagues, direct reports or others to achieve business outcomes.
5. _5_ She keeps her co-workers, direct reports or others in her process chain aligned on key strategic goals.
6. _5_ She has strong internal and external strategic networks that she taps in service of business outcomes.
7. _6_ She is able to speak knowledgeably about the business and presents herself with confidence.
8. _1_ She leads from a clear sense of purpose and in alignment with her values.
9. _7_ She is clear about, confident in and able to leverage her personal strengths.

Questions 1–3 relate to achieving and sustaining extraordinary outcomes. If you scored below 7 in any one of these three questions, you'll want to pay particular attention to Section 1: Achieve and Sustain Extraordinary Outcomes.

Questions 4–6 relate to engaging and aligning others. If you scored below a 7 in any one of these three questions, you'll find Section 2 on Engage the Greatness in Others most helpful.

Questions 7–9 relate to leading from your personal greatness. If you scored below a 7 in any one of these three questions, you'll want to put a special focus on Section 3: Use Personal Greatness.

Reading forward, I will especially focus on:

_____

_____

_____

_____

_____

_____

_____

_____

_____

_____

Achieve and Sustain
Extraordinary Outcomes

In many ways, achieving and sustaining extraordinary outcomes is the hidden element of leadership for women. Because many models of leadership are rooted in the 1970s and based on studies of men, conventional wisdom on leadership has tended to ignore *outcomes* to focus instead on individual attributes or interpersonal skills. And, as we discussed in Part One, leading for outcomes is an area where bosses consistently rank men as outperforming women.

This makes leading for outcomes one of the most important leadership concepts for women. Lack of understanding in this area causes the greatest drag on women's progress up the organization. That's why this section of the book includes five chapters — some rather long — and a substantial number of Lead ON! activities.

Because this section addresses the Missing 33%, which is so crucial to women's success, I've put it first. I hope you will read and re-read these chapters and use the Lead ON! activities until you can naturally incorporate into your daily actions the concepts and language of outcomes.

Lead for Outcomes

What do we mean by *outcome?* This is a hugely important question because many of us tend to think of our jobs in terms of the question, "What do I do every day?" instead of, "Why does the company pay for my job to exist?" The result is that many of us think of our job as a collection of *activities* instead of as a demand to deliver *outcomes.* To understand what I mean by this, let's differentiate between four concepts: inputs, activities, results and outcomes:

- **Inputs:** are resources used to support activities, e.g. money, people, materials.
- **Activities:** are projects, programs, initiatives or steps in a process that are undertaken for their positive impact on outcomes.
- **Results:** are the measurable parameters of *activities.* They contribute to, but aren't the same as, outcomes.
- **Outcomes:** are the direct measurable impact on the organization's financial targets and strategic outcomes in

the areas of cash, growth, return and customer — more about these in the next chapter.

To illustrate the differences, consider these two projects. One is to develop a computer system. The other is a construction project. Both have inputs, activities, results and outcomes.

	Develop and implement a computer system to pay disability claims.	Build and open a new hospital emergency department (ED).
Inputs	Hardware, development software, people, budgeted dollars, user specifications	The budgeted capital dollars, construction materials, people working on the project, and the design plans
Activities	Project planning, coding, system testing, user testing, parallel testing	Creating the blueprints, constructing the addition, training staff, ordering equipment and stocking supplies are all examples of activities involved in building a new ED.
Results	System is implemented on or ahead of schedule and on or under budget. Performance meets all testing and other thresholds.	ED is opened on schedule and at or under budget. Related training was conducted on schedule, new equipment installed on schedule and performs to standards. Building passes fire safety requirements.
Outcomes	Ineligible claim payments are reduced, saving the company millions of dollars. Customer satisfaction rates increase because payments are more accurate. New business increases 15%.	The projected increase in patient visits is being met. Targets for additional revenue are being met. Patient satisfaction scores have increased.

If you're finding the distinction between *results* and *outcomes* confusing, here's a further explanation of the difference: *Results* are interim measures. They often support the attainment of *outcomes*, but are not in and of themselves outcomes. For example, the decision to build a new emergency department (ED) is made because management believes that it will favorably impact outcomes by generating additional *revenue* (through greater volume of patients treated in the ED and through increased patients admitted to the hospital through the ED). The building project has a defined budget and deadline. If the ED is completed on time and within budget, it achieves the interim *results*. But if it doesn't deliver the expected *revenue*, it isn't hitting *outcomes*. So, if you're the project manager, beware of resting on your laurels if you've done your job (opened on time and on budget) but not delivered the expected outcomes.

As a leader, how do you *achieve and sustain extraordinary outcomes?* Let's start by explaining what are NOT extraordinary outcomes.

Extraordinary outcomes are NOT about maintaining the status quo or delivering the inevitable. Maintaining the status quo will cause the organization to fall behind in its rapidly changing external environment. In spite of the fact that many executives preside over the decline of their organization, this is not leadership. Delivering the inevitable means that the result would have happened without your intervention. That doesn't count as leadership, either.

Similarly, an extraordinary outcome is not the result of a random occurrence or luck. For example, if a competitor leaves your market enabling your team to exceed its sales goals, you don't get to take credit for leadership.

And "flash in the pan" outcomes don't count — no matter how extraordinary. Think of Lee Iacocca, who engineered a remarkable but unsustainable turnaround at Chrysler. Remember our definition of leadership includes the word *sustain*. True leadership means delivering outcomes over time.

Finally, extraordinary isn't about effort invested. In other words, it's not about how hard you work. Let me say this again: It's not about how hard you work or how many hours you put in. I have a favorite quote that makes this point beautifully:

"No one cares the storms you encounter,
they only care did you bring in the ship."

—Anonymous

This is another area where women shoot ourselves in the foot. So often when we're asked, "How are you?" we answer with some version of, "I'm so busy." Think about this for a minute. When you declare you're busy, you're telegraphing your inability to do the job you have, so why would anyone think of advancing you to a higher position? Don't ever say you're busy! Instead, say you're enjoying the challenge of XX project, or seeing great progress on YY initiative, or just coming from reporting to your team how they hit all of their outcome goals.

Aside from "bringing in the ship," what makes an outcome *extraordinary?* It's pretty simple. **To deliver an extraordinary outcome, you must help the organization hit or exceed goals that it defines as important for its vitality and growth.** Here's how Susan Arnold describes her ascension to president of global business units at Proctor & Gamble. *"I was able to attain my current position for two reasons. First, I delivered excellent results. As a vice president, I oversaw multiple businesses in beauty care and* **led our largest profit center in North America to the best [outcomes] we'd had in a decade.** *Second, I had great advocacy at the top..."*

In other words, what makes an outcome extraordinary is that it is aligned with your organization's strategy. To lead for outcomes, you'll need business acumen, strategic acumen and financial acumen. These are what we cover in the next chapters, beginning with business acumen.

▶ **Lead ON!**

Understanding *Outcomes*

It's important that you understand the difference between inputs, activities, results and outcomes. Use the chart below to test your understanding. Indicate whether each statement refers to an input (I), activity (A), result (R) or outcome (O).

O	*We achieved patient satisfaction scores of 98% last quarter.*
	1. We invested $1.3 million in the technology and infrastructure.
	2. The team will create an automated system to pay Long Term Disability claims.
	3. Nationwide, the 10-person team directed 250 people.
	4. The new information system reduced time-to-customer-payment by three weeks.
	5. The streamlined process reduced staff, saving 25% of salaries and benefit costs.
	6. The new office is a $15-million project.
	7. The customer information tracking system was the first in the company to be completed both on time and within budget.
	8. The new claim system saved $300,000 a month by eliminating payments to non-eligible claimants.
	9. The patient documentation system reduced medication errors by 85%.
	10. The new emergency department (ED) will handle an additional 15,000 patient visits/year.

See answers on the next page

Answers

Input — focuses on the *resources* invested.	1. We invested $1.3 million in the technology and infrastructure.
Activities — describes a *project*.	2. The team will create an automated system to pay Long Term Disability claims.
Input — describes the *resources* of the project.	3. Nationwide, the 10-person project team directed 250 people.
Result — by reducing the time a customer has to wait for payment, the *result* will be increased customer satisfaction. However, this doesn't measure customer satisfaction.	4. The new information system reduced the time-to-customer-payment by three weeks.
Outcome — describes direct impact on costs (therefore, *Return*).	5. The streamlined process reduced staff, saving 25% of salaries and benefit costs.
Input — focuses on the *resources* required to build the office.	6. The new office is a $15-million project.
Result — describes the *parameters* met by the activity.	7. The customer information tracking system was the first in the company to be completed both on time and within budget.
Outcome — describes direct impact on costs (therefore, *Return*).	8. The new claim system saved $300,000 a month by eliminating payments to non-eligible claimants.
Outcome — describes direct impact on *Customer* — service quality.	9. The patient documentation system reduced medication errors by 85%.
You could argue whether this is a Result or an Outcome. Patient visits directly translate into revenue, which would make this an outcome. A more targeted outcome statement would be: *The additional 15,000 ED patient visits will generate $500,000 in revenue.*	10. The new emergency department (ED) will handle an additional 15,000 patient visits/year.

Think Like a CEO:
Business Acumen

"Women are not yet claiming the corner office because they are not getting experience in the business of the business. This is the key that will unlock the doors for women throughout corporate America."
—SHEILA WELLINGTON, PRESIDENT
CATALYST

Julie Hill, CEO of Costain Homes and director of WellPoint, Inc. (among other companies), won her CEO position over three men because of her business acumen. She and the three men were called to meet with the British parent of Costain after the ousting of its American president. During the meetings, the men were at a loss to answer general questions about the health of the business as a whole. Julie, on the other hand, wowed them with her breadth of understanding about the business, its vision and plan.

The earlier in your career you learn the business of your business — what makes it successful and how you support/drive the organization's success — the better. I call this **business acumen and it means understanding the four outcome categories that tell the story of your organization's health: cash, growth, return and customer.**

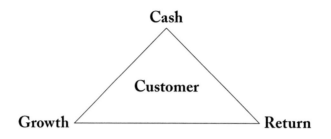

These four areas are core whether you work in a for-profit or not-for-profit organization. In government organizations, the measures are slightly different, but basic concepts are the same. If you have business acumen — no matter your level — you understand the relationships between these four areas and place appropriate focus on each. Here's what you need to know.

Cash

Organizations focus on two key, cash-related measures. The amount of cash on hand is usually measured and reported as *days cash on hand*. This indicates how long the business could run without one penny of additional revenue. Cash on hand is important because it enables the company to make money passively through investments and interest earned. Cash on hand also represents a safety net, and a large safety net means that a lender can reasonably expect to be repaid. That's why cash on hand influences an organization's bond ratings and the interest rate at which it can borrow.

There's another reason why cash on hand is important. It is a source for funding growth — whether through acquisition, expansion or new product introduction. A few years ago, Home Depot had to stop building new stores because its growth was running ahead of its ability to generate cash. And when the auto industry went to Congress for assistance at the end of 2008, you heard over and over that they were "burning through cash" — there were no reserves to fuel growth (not to mention maintain current operations).

When Mary Sammons became CEO of Rite Aid, the company was failing. She had an operational plan for turning around the company. What she discovered was there was no cash on hand. In a 2007 *WSJ* interview, she said, *"I was looking at the cash sheet every day, just to make sure there was a little bit of cash there."* Without it, she was unable to execute the turnaround plan she had developed. Her primary challenge became one of cash generation.

The *speed of cash generation* is an efficiency indicator. It indicates how quickly a product or service is converted into revenue. Shortening the number of days between when an invoice is issued and the money is collected (AR Days) is very important because it means more cash on hand more quickly.

Before the financial meltdown of 2008–09, many executives were focused on growth and return. As credit dried up, focus increasingly shifted to cash. Knowledge of how much cash can be generated from core business operations, what can be obtained from other sources and how much cash had to be paid out became crucial information. Even if return is looking good, lack of cash or decreasing cash is a red flag.

If you think about different functions in organizations, it's easy to see that you can lead for cash-related outcomes if you are in the billing or accounts receivable, sales, inventory management or handle invest-ments. But, in fact, all functions indirectly impact cash through the expenses they incur. Any time you or your staff conserve resources, you potentially increase money that could go from profit to cash on hand.

Growth

Growth is the lifeblood of any company, and a focus on growth is the hallmark of great CEOs. **Growth is achieved through new or enhanced products or services reaching new customers, moves into new markets (for example, regions or countries) and through merg-ers and acquisitions.** Numeric measures in the area of growth are usually reported as percent of market share, overall revenue growth, same-store sales and other similar measures.

But not all growth is equal. **To really lead for growth, organiza-tions need *profitable* growth.** Growth that is unprofitable or outstrips cash generation (as described earlier with Home Depot) is dangerous for the health of the organization.

Consider again Anne Mulcahy, former CEO of Xerox. When she took over, consultants advised that if the company were to cut R&D and engineering funding, it would be able to immediately generate cash and profit. But, as Xerox CEO Ursula Burns explains, even in the darkest time they made the decision to not cut R&D spending because they knew that, at its core, Xerox was a technology company. They continued to invest in innovation at the same rate even during the troubled times. She says, "*...we kept whole our greatest growth lever, our technology.*" The result? In 2008, she could say about Xerox's growth that they "*launched over 100 new products in the last three years and two-thirds of Xerox revenue in any given year is generated from a product launched less than two years before...revenue is growing...and we delivered double-digit earnings.*"

At Hewlett Packard (H-P), former CEO Carly Fiorina faced a situation of undisciplined investment in growth. "*We were a company that had always celebrated invention and yet we no longer invented. Our annual patent production lagged behind others...didn't measure our innovation, and no one could tell me how many patents we produced. We had no sense of the productivity of our R&D resources.*" She understood that innovation without discipline and commercialization were hallmarks of unsustainable growth.

You can lead for growth-related outcomes if you're working in areas such as new product development, business development, research, marketing, strategic planning, M&A or sales. Or, if you're thinking great thoughts about what your customers want. One mid-level manager I know proposed a new service line that was fully funded in a tough economy because the potential return on investment was so great (you'll read about her in the chapter Show Me the Money). As a matter of fact, even if you're in HR, you can lead for outcomes in this area by ensuring that sales compensation rewards profitable sales.

Return

For the sake of simplicity, we'll talk about return as a function of two elements: **margin** and **velocity**. A formula for calculating return is:

Margin × Velocity = Return

Margin (sometimes called profit) is comprised of two elements, revenue/income and expenses/costs. When Anne Moore, CEO of Time, Inc., says, *"I care about two things going forward, get the cost out, grow revenue,"* she is hitting on these two elements. A simple calculation for margin is:

Revenue − Expenses = Margin

Basically, any organization wants a margin. For-profit companies like margins in the double-digits, not-for-profits set more modest goals.

Putting both of these concepts together, we get:

(Revenue — Expenses) × Velocity = Return

Velocity refers to how quickly things are done. This is one of the reasons why in all types of organizations there's been so much focus on process improvement initiatives.

In manufacturing organizations, the faster the inventory turn, the higher the velocity. When Ursula Burns, CEO of Xerox, speaks about the Xerox turnaround, she makes the point that they began with $2.6 billion in inventory turning at about two times per year. By 2008, they had reduced inventory to $1.1 billion and increased inventory turns to five times per year (though proud of the progress, she concedes that this is still nowhere near greatness).

But anything that is done more quickly contributes to return. This is why companies place such a strong emphasis on productivity. If your organization has used automation to speed up a previously manual process or if you've found a way to get work done more quickly, you've experienced increased velocity.

You can lead for improved return by increasing revenue, decreasing expenses and/or increasing velocity. People in sales have an obvious opportunity to lead for revenue generation. But, you can lead for positive return no matter where you work in an organization because no matter where in the organization you work, you can identify or make a change to increase efficiency (velocity). Angela Ahrendts, CEO of Burberry, is a case in point. Early in her career, when working for Donna Karan, she increased the delivery rate on booked orders from around 75% to 95% by improving the efficiency of the production and distribution system.

You can also lead for positive return no matter where you work by finding ways to reduce expenses. But beware of an over-focus on expense reduction. As Kathleen Hittner, CEO of The Miriam Hospital (TMH), has said, *"You can't shrink your way to greatness."* If you pay close attention to the stories of cost cutting by well-run organizations, you will find that savings are directed to cash or invested in growth, not to maintain operations.

Sandra Cheng, VP of TMH, provides an example of this. Sandra oversees facilities, dietary, housekeeping, volunteers, the call center and other non-medical functions. Nevertheless, in a meeting with the CEO of Lifespan (of which TMH is a member), she proposed and got approval to research the viability of implementing a system that would allow patients to make their own appointments and to make them at their own convenience without being tied to the hospital's business hours. By decreasing the cost of making patient appointments, all the hospitals in the Lifespan system would have additional resources to devote toward new patient care services.

If you work in a not-for-profit or governmental organization, the concept of return is not that different. In spite of their names, even not-for-profits must have a profit or margin. When they have a margin, they have money available for reinvestment in infrastructure (for example, new facilities or capital equipment), new programs for clients or benefits for staff. Any well-run not-for-profit, no matter how well endowed, will work to avoid multiple years of deficit. For governments, a balanced budget is a goal (or a mandate). Monies for reinvestment and growth are budgeted in the front end as an expense.

In all cases, improvements in velocity (productivity) are important to help deliver services at the lowest possible cost. And boards of directors and taxpayers care about this.

Whether you work for public, private or not-for-profit organizations, it's important to lead for positive return.

Customer...and Consumer

The three outcome categories discussed so far — cash, growth and return — are part of an important cycle. Profitable growth fuels return, return fuels cash, and cash fuels growth.

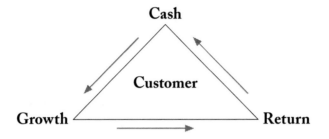

This virtuous cycle is only possible if there's a satisfied customer standing at the center of the enterprise. This satisfied customer is, simply put, your company's source of revenue. Without customers, there is no business. **Customers are the heart of a business and great leaders understand how to acquire and stay close to them.**

Anne Mulcahy understood that rebuilding relationships with customers was necessary for Xerox's future. Not only did she go on the road to meet with key customers, she also held each of her executives accountable for relationships with at least one of its top 500 customers. Ursula Burns has said that one of Xerox's key learnings from the turnaround was that the *"customer is the center of just about everything... employees will lose jobs if we forget about the customer, shareholders will lose value...the brand will definitely deteriorate...the firm will spiral out of control if you forget about the customer. You have to remember who you're serving and make sure that 99 percent of your decisions are focused on who you are serving."*

Ann Livermore, Executive Vice President of Hewlett-Packard's storage and servers, software and services businesses, makes it a practice to speak with two or three big customers every day and to use their input and other information to spot market trends and shape strategy. She describes how conversations with customers influenced H-P's strategic deal with EDS. *"I was talking to two large financial institutions, a manufacturing company and a government organization that all had very large IT outsourcing opportunities for us, but we didn't have the resources to respond. By combining our outsourcing business with EDS, we'll have tremendous scale and be able to respond to every opportunity."* Seeing the customer need and the market opportunity, Ann then worked with H-P CEO Mark Hurd to develop the strategy for the EDS deal.

Being close to and understanding customer and consumer needs is essential to being able to develop business acumen and think like a CEO. No matter what function you're in, you can find ways to understand the customer experience. Shadow a service technician, tag along on a sales call, visit one of your stores or ask a salesperson to explain your product. There are a myriad of ways. If you worked for Proctor & Gamble, you might even be sent anywhere in the world to live with prospective consumers!

Among the tools for understanding the customer are measurements of **three customer-related outcomes: acquiring customers, serving them and retaining them**. Retention is particularly important. Research repeatedly finds that if you can retain 5% more of your existing customers, you can increase profit by 25% to 50%. Additionally, it takes five times more money and effort to attract a new customer than to retain an existing customer. So, while it's essential to attract new customers, it is unwise to do that at the expense of losing existing customers. In the customer space, smart organizations measure both acquisition and retention rates in addition to customer service metrics that relate to product quality, product safety and customer satisfaction.

Identifying your customer is not always simple. **Many organizations face the challenges of developing internal capability to serve both *customers* and *consumers*.** Simply stated, the customer is who pays your company for its product or service. Your customer may or may not use the product or service. The consumer is the one who uses the product or service and does not pay you directly. Take the example of Proctor & Gamble. P&G makes all kinds of products, from soaps to face cream to baby diapers.

P&G serves *consumers* — you and me — by creating products that we want to use. They have elaborate internal processes for identifying and developing new products that we'll want to buy. They live with consumers, hold focus groups, apply science to packaging design, etc. They also have to serve the *customers* who pay them directly — retailers such as Target, CVS/Caremark, WalMart and your local convenience or grocery store — by creating processes that make it easy for these retailers to order, display and pay for their products.

Let's look at a non-profit example — a school that educates children with disabilities. The children and their families rarely pay the full cost of these services. The revenue comes from state agencies and school districts. So, like P&G, this non-profit must meet the needs of both *customers* (those who provide direct revenue) and *consumers* (the children they educate).

There exists a pervasive yet questionable notion that people within your company can be customers. I get on a soapbox about this because the idea of "internal customers" has significantly reduced fundamental business understanding — something we as women can't afford. It is more useful to think of the people you serve within the company as "co-creators of the value streams that exist to serve your paying customers and consumers." You don't have to call your co-creators "customers" in order to deliver the highest service and quality to them. If you recognize how important they are to your real customers, this alone should drive you to deliver to them the best service you can — while keeping your eyes on your real customers and consumers!

The most direct opportunities to lead for customer outcomes are in functions like sales, customer service, distribution, product design, product safety and product quality.

New Perspectives

Recently, boards have begun looking beyond the four traditional outcome areas of cash, growth, return and customer. Recognizing that short-term stock market returns don't tell the whole story of organizational success and that factors like employee engagement and sustainable business practices influence long-term success, they have begun to ask CEOs to report on two other areas: **compliance & community** and **capability.** I sometimes depict these six elements like this:

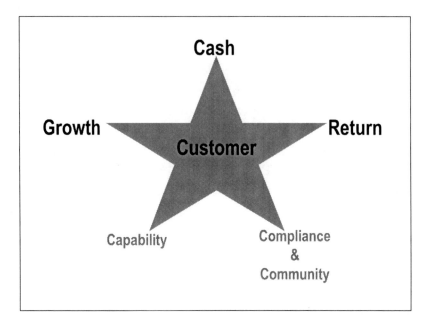

Capability refers to the organization's internal ability to execute its strategy. It includes infrastructure, people and processes. When companies measure employee engagement, they are quantifying a *capability* measure. Questions about whether a plant can handle increased production to support a move into a new market would be a capability-related question. In the capability space, boards are increasingly asking about company morale, risk management plans and organizational flexibility and agility. Functions that influence capability include marketing, HR, IT, process engineering, facilities, risk management and training & development/OD.

Even if you directly lead for outcomes in the area of capability, it's important to understand how your area drives results in the four core outcome areas. For example, developing a recruitment process that results in high-quality hires who stay for several years has a positive impact on return and on growth if they are new hires required to support a growth strategy. Building a new plant drives the opportunity to contribute to growth and return.

Boards are increasingly concerned with whether organizations are meeting regulatory constraints placed upon them (think government regulations, industry standards). At the same time, some are increasingly pressuring organizations to look toward green and sustainability practices because they recognize that climate change and unsustainable practices influence the marketplace and present opportunities for efficiencies. Thirdly, some boards pay particular attention to company image — which can be strongly influenced by its track record in the community and on environmental and human issues. Functions that influence compliance and community issues include legal, compliance, sustainability and community social responsibility.

Again, **if you're working in a Compliance & Community function, it's essential that you are able to draw a straight line to how your compliance or community-related activities support the four core business outcomes.** This is a point Irene Rosenfeld, CEO of Kraft Foods, made in a speech on sustainability and Kraft's environmental efforts. She attributed the failure of Kraft's earlier efforts to the lack of a business proposition. She went on to say about recent efforts, *"You can do well by doing good. The key is to make sure you have a **business purpose** that is in line with the societal opportunity and that you have some clear metrics and milestones along the way."* In other words, successful sustainability practices emerge and persist not only because they are the right thing to do, but also because they drive cash, growth, return and customer outcomes.

Your Positional Purpose

Leaders understand the difference between "doing your job" and "leading for outcomes." In this way, they stay focused on what I call their *positional purpose*. I first understood the importance of positional purpose when I heard about a CEO who would join a random group of employees for lunch in the cafeteria and ask, "What do I pay you to do here?" Simply answering, "I'm in the accounting department" or "I'm a programmer" was not what he was looking for. He was asking whether the employees understood why there was a salary allocated for their position. In other words, among the four outcomes, which did the employee impact. This is your positional purpose.

For example, the positional purpose of a customer-service manager is to make sure that customers receive excellent service. This position leads for customer-related outcomes — specifically service and retention. At the same time, service excellence reduces the costs of regrettable loss of customers and lowers customer acquisition costs. So, the customer-service manager also drives return, which fuels cash and creates a brand identity that supports profitable growth.

Here's another example. The positional purpose of a VP of HR includes ensuring that there are employees with the knowledge and skills to support planned growth and deliver appropriate service (either directly or by supporting the customer-facing staff). Her job is to lead for outcomes in the areas of growth and customer. Doing this in an efficient way drives return.

A manufacturing site manager for a global enterprise exists to drive positive outcomes in the areas of return and customer by ensuring manufacturing efficiency and product quality. A sales VP is paid to drive growth, return and customer outcomes by making sure that customer acquisition is seamless, growth targets are met and growth is profitable.

Clarity about your positional purpose helps you lead in your current position by being able to differentiate between more important and less important work. It helps you speak more authoritatively about what you do and why you do it. It helps you position yourself as having business acumen in addition to your professional expertise. Billie Williamson, America's director of flexibility and gender equity at Ernst & Young, learned that the answer to "What do I pay you to do around here?" isn't "I'm an accountant." She spent 20 of her early years at E&Y as an auditor and left to join a hi-tech company in the CFO position to help take it public. She then moved to Marriott International as SVP of finance. When she came back to E&Y, she said about her external positions, *"Leaving for a while gave me* *the credentials to be a **business executive**, not just an accountant.*" The experiences helped her realize how to fulfill her positional purpose. You don't have to move to a new company, though. You can begin to hone your business acumen and define your positional purpose right where you are.

▶ Lead ON!

Understanding Cash, Growth, Return and Customer

If you have opportunities to attend or watch your CEO report to the board or to employees, or to read transcripts of quarterly reports to shareholders or have other opportunities to hear business updates, take them. Then map his/her comments to cash, growth, return, customer. If you can't get your hands on your CEO's update, take this quiz (psst, there may be more than one correct response):

1. Which of the following statements from CEOs' reports to their boards relate to CASH?
   A. Accounts Receivable days declined from 93 to 41 over the past five years.
   B. Our gross revenue exceeded $541 million.
   C. Customer satisfaction scores as reported by JD Powers remain in the 90th percentile.
   D. Days cash on hand increased to 935.

2. Which of the following statements from CEOs' reports to their boards relate to GROWTH?
   A. Patient satisfaction scores have increased from the 83rd percentile to the 88th.
   B. Investment Returns outperformed the market in every quarter.
   C. Opening of new buildings enabled us to increase patient volume from 9,000 visits per year to more than 15,000.
   D. Same-store sales increased by 13%.

3. Which of the following statements from CEOs' reports to
   their boards relate to RETURN?
   - A. Operating expenses declined quarter over quarter.
   - B. Revenue for the 3rd quarter increased 23%.
   - C. We've invested $15 million in new technology to
     improve patient safety.
   - D. Inventory turns have increased 40% as a result of our
     lean manufacturing initiatives.

4. Which of the following statements from CEOs' reports to
   their boards relate to CUSTOMER?
   - A. We've reduced customer complaints about quality
     by 80%.
   - B. Our net margin was $27 billion.
   - C. Customer satisfaction scores as reported by JD Powers
     remain in the 90th percentile.
   - D. Days cash on hand decreased to 547.

Answers:

1. A and D

2. C and D

3. A and B

4. A and C

Define Your Positional Purpose

Now that you've got these concepts down pat, you're ready to
define your Positional Purpose and map your responsibilities to key
outcomes. Use the **Positional Purpose Worksheet** at our website,
www.NoCeilingNoWalls.com.

Business Acumen @ Every Level

In addition to knowing your Positional Purpose, here are other ways
you can develop and demonstrate Business Acumen @ Every Level.

As an **individual contributor:**
- Develop business acumen by learning how your work fits into the overall flow of the business and how the metrics that you have to meet contribute to overall organizational performance. You can do this by asking your supervisor/ manager, a mentor and your colleagues from other parts of the business. You'll also find clues in reports given by senior management.
- Demonstrate business acumen by describing your contribution to *outcomes* when it's time for you to talk with your supervisor/manager about your performance.

As a **supervisor/manager,** in addition to the above, you can begin to:
- Develop business acumen further by looking beyond your team(s) to identify interdependence with others outside your area. Develop relationships across functions to understand how they contribute to the business.
- Demonstrate it by acting on the interdependence to promote cross-functional innovations and improvements justified by robust ROI analyses.
- Demonstrate it by motivating people to change their behavior to hit key metrics.

Carrying your earlier knowledge and actions forward as **senior manager,** take advantage of opportunities to further:
- Develop business acumen by attending board meetings and paying attention to the questions that board members ask. With an executive mentor, analyze the *"why"* behind the questions. Pay attention to the executives who are presenting and ask *why* their presentations are structured as they are, how and *why* they touch upon cash, growth, return and customer.
- Demonstrate business acumen not only by hitting key outcomes, but also by presenting strategic recommendations with full ROI analyses in a board-friendly format.

If you've cultivated your business acumen at earlier levels, at the **executive level** it should be fairly strong. Now you can capitalize on the opportunity to:

- Demonstrate your business acumen through your executive impact on operations and the bottom line — including decisions you make and the strategic initiatives you propose, approve and execute — and through your reports to the board.
- If necessary, get coaching to ensure that your presentations to the board summarize major issues and opportunities as directors want to see/hear them: high level with stated impact on cash, growth, return, customer.

At the **board level,** you demonstrate business acumen by being able to analyze financial reports for what they tell you about the current and future health of the organization and it's alignment (or not) with its strategy. You evaluate proposals and other board documents from the strategic level for their short- and long-term impact on cash, growth, return, customer, capability and compliance and community. If you want to develop further business acumen, find a director who is a role model for business acumen (possibly on a different board) and ask for assistance.

Prioritize Your Time

Make sure you invest time and energy on activities that have the greatest direct impact on key outcomes instead of those with indirect or no impact on key outcomes (no matter how much more enjoyable they might be). For example:

Instead of...	Consider ...
Answering all e-mails or voice mails in chronological order.	Prioritizing each message by its connection to key outcomes and answering only the most important.
Chatting about random things with co-workers and staff.	Adding a focus on outcomes. Ask for updates, praise on progress or coaching on issues.

My opportunity for increased focus:

Doing other things before group notes.	Complete notes right after group if possible. Do 1 group at a time, then take breaks & other tasks.
Have a to-do list	Prioritize by days.

Chart a Course: Strategic Acumen

"It isn't necessary that you be a CEO to seek the big picture."
—Ram Charan

Do you know what strategy is? How about why it's set? Do you know why boards are interested in strategy? Can you describe the relationship between strategy and business outcomes? If you can answer all these questions, you might have strategic acumen (if you're an executive and are making poor strategic choices in spite of answering "yes," you don't quite have it). If not, that's what you'll get out of this chapter. And, you'll understand how you can develop and exhibit strategic acumen at every level.

Hold onto your hats (do women even wear hats anymore?). This chapter is as long as it is important!

The What and *Why* of Strategy

My favorite question when I work with women to build strategic acumen is, "Why do boards exist?" Most often the responses I hear include: to hire and fire CEOs, monitor performance, approve strategy or ensure resource availability. These describe the *activities* of a board. They answer the question of "what" boards do, but they don't quite answer the question of "why" boards exist.

Boards exist to represent the interests of external stakeholders. For-profit directors stand in place of shareholders to ensure that the

79

company is well run, profitable and viable into the future. Not-for-profit boards stand in place of the community to ensure that the organization is well run, able to create sufficient margin for reinvestment and that it is viable into the future in order to continue delivering important community services. Therefore, one of a board's responsibilities is to ensure that management has a *strategy* that ensures profitability, growth and future viability.

This is the point that Patricia Russo, CEO of Alcatel-Lucent, makes when she says, *"I could have done a lot of things to make next year better in the short term but part of my job is to ensure a sustainable good future for the company. I tried to come up with the best plan for our long-term success."* She could have made the short-term look rosy, but she couldn't take actions that would threaten Alcatel-Lucent's long-term viability.

Holding simultaneous focus on the long- and short-term is one of a leader's balancing acts — and it is expected of executives. Recently, Patricia Woertz, CEO of Archer Daniels Midland, described herself as using *"bifocal vision"* to keep focused on both long- and short-term trends.

To ensure this balanced focus on the short- and long-terms, all well-run organizations, including not-for-profits, have a board-approved strategy. Sometimes the strategy is explicit, sometimes it's implicitly reflected in its financial targets. So, what is a strategy? I like to use this definition from Larry Bossidy and Ram Charan's book, *Execution*,

> "[strategy is the means for a company]...*to win the customer's preference and create a sustainable competitive advantage while leaving enough money on the table for shareholders."*

In the case of not-for-profits, strategy leaves enough money on the table for reinvestment. So a **strategy must do three things — each of which aligns with the four outcome areas covered in the prior chapter:**

1. Win the customer's preference. (CUSTOMER)

2. Create a sustainable competitive advantage. (GROWTH)
3. Leave money on the table. (CASH and RETURN)

Andrea Jung took over at Avon in 1999 when the company was failing to meet its quarterly earning target. By late 2006, Avon had eliminated 10% of the workforce, 15% of management and reduced the hierarchy from 15 levels to eight. The result? $200 million in savings annually (fueling CASH). Why did she want to save that much money? To make the following *strategic* moves:

1. Fund significant investments in product innovation (a $100 million R&D center) (GROWTH and CUSTOMER),
2. Increase efficiency through increased internet presence — especially in international markets (for example, Turkey where 95% of sales were made by representatives using internet cafes) (RETURN), and
3. Expand into new markets such as China, India, Russia and Brazil where per person spending on beauty lags far behind that in developed countries (GROWTH).

Avon's moves illustrate that the process of developing/changing strategy is an iterative process based on an analysis of the external marketplace, outcomes the company must hit (especially financial targets) and the company's internal capabilities. The CEO is expected to deliver to the board financial targets that will ensure viability by keeping the company out of the "red zone of failure" and to deliver on those targets. What do I mean by the "red zone of failure"? To answer, let's first explore why leadership is about all change, all the time.

All Change, All the Time

In 1989, noted leadership expert Warren Bennis claimed, *"Learning to lead is **on one level** learning to manage change."* It would be more accurate to say that, *"Learning to lead **is on every level** learning to manage change."* Change is #1 on the agenda of CEOs of well-performing companies and anyone else at any level who wants to think like a CEO. Here's why.

As illustrated in the diagram below, the rate of change in the marketplace and in consumer expectations is increasing at a rapid rate — and some say at an increasingly rapid rate. If an organization were to deliver future performance that is no better or only marginally better than it's current performance, it would inevitably enter the red zone of failure. Organizations of whatever size (from work team to global enterprise) fall behind if they perform at current levels. As George Vecchione, CEO of Lifespan, has said, *"Just to stay where we are, we have to be getting better."*

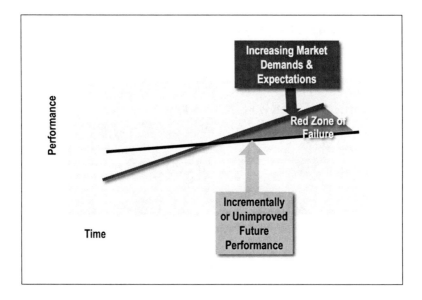

Once in the red zone of failure, an organization is no longer providing what its customers want at prices they're willing to pay. Think PanAm, American Motors, Firestone, Chrysler or GM. At one point or another, these large American companies were at the top of their industries. All are gone or in trouble. Some were sold off. Others went bankrupt. They each entered the red zone of failure.

Several F500 organizations were in or on the edge of the red zone of failure when women were appointed CEO. Carol Bartz at Yahoo!, Anne Mulcahy at Xerox, Andrea Jung at Avon, Brenda Barnes at Sara Lee, Mary Sammons at Rite-Aid and Carly Fiorina at H-P are but a few examples. This is such a noteworthy phenomenon that there is a term for it: "glass cliff," describing when a woman is at high risk of failure because she was promoted to CEO at a time when a company is in crisis. Obviously, the number one item on their agenda would have to be change — change to save their faltering companies.

How did they reposition their companies? They asked, "What new level of performance will lift the organization out of the red zone of failure?"

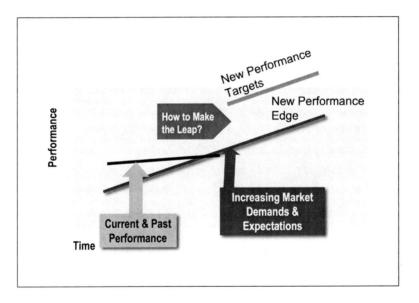

They established financial targets and other strategic goals for that level of performance. In other words, they set strategy. Inevitably, these new performance goals require that the organization change.

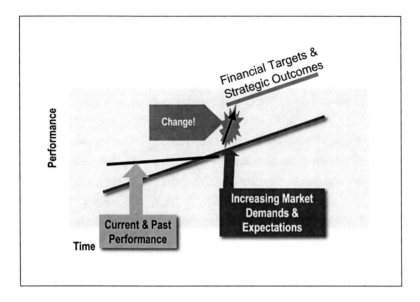

They then managed the organizational changes required to shift performance to the new levels. For Avon, this meant investment in R&D for the development of new revenue-boosting products, efficiency improvements to increase return and infrastructure changes necessary for expansion into new countries to drive growth.

You see similar moves being made at Sunoco where, shortly after her appointment as CEO, Lynn Elsenhans announced several management changes that would position the company for stronger performance and growth. Discussing Sunoco's external environment, she said, *"Volatility in crude oil markets, changing demand for gasoline and distillate products and new refining capacity being added throughout the world mean that Sunoco has to take steps now to strengthen its position for long-term growth."* She then went on to announce management changes: the SVP of Business Improvement was charged with a *"new company-wide effort to improve Sunoco's cost structure and business process efficiency"* (increase RETURN — to generate additional cash for growth) and the SVP of Strategy and Portfolio will focus on *"developing strategic options...including joint ventures, mergers, acquisitions* (GROWTH) *and divestitures* (to generate CASH and increase RETURN).

You can see that **to avoid the red zone of failure, leadership is all about all change, all the time — no matter your level.** At any level, you might feel the impact of strategy as it is executed (think a reorganization, new process, new computer system, reduction in force or merger/acquisition). As an individual contributor, you exercise strategic thinking when you look for opportunities to improve your and your colleagues' work processes. As a supervisor, you contribute to strategy execution by enabling your team to change to meet ever-increasing performance goals. As a manager, you import innovation, master process change and lead for change across multiple teams and functions. And, as an executive, you set and execute strategy to position your organization for success in the rapidly changing marketplace. Leadership is all change, all the time, and your organization's strategy is its means for dealing with and creating change in the marketplace.

To keep the company ahead of market demands, the CEO develops strategy (codified in its financial targets), presents it to the board, and then reports on progress to the board and for public companies to shareholders. This is why a company's reports to Wall Street are so important. They signal whether the company is delivering on its strategy; in other words, whether it will win the customer's preference, create a sustainable advantage and leave money on the table.

At its simplest level, there are only so many strategic moves a company can make. These include:

Growth Initiatives, such as:
- Product/service innovation or new products/services
- Merger/acquisition
- Expansion into new markets

Customer Initiatives, including:
- Product quality/safety initiatives (e.g. SixSigma)
- Service excellence initiatives

Return/Cash Initiatives, for example:

- Expense management (supply chain management, off-shoring, layoffs)
- Revenue enhancement (revenue cycle management)
- Process improvement initiatives (e.g. lean manufacturing)

Strategy formulation is an iterative and interdependent process. The three essential factors are the organization's financial position and targets, the external marketplace and its internal capabilities. Here's what I mean. Put yourself in the shoes of the CEO. An analysis of the market indicates that your company can realistically capture 35% market share over three years. Your growth target for year one is 10% and cash flow goals are set based on that target. During the year you see that you're going to fall short. To figure out why and what actions to take, you analyze the external market, your financial goals and internal capability. Was the 10% target missed because the market changed or because of an internal deficit (e.g. inadequate sales skills, insufficient marketing/advertising, poor product quality and deteriorating reputation)? Based on the analysis, what will the impact on next year's financial targets be — cash flow and market share?

Your Strategy Mentor: Anne Mulcahy, Xerox

Now that I've mentioned it several times, let's look in some detail at the turnaround of Xerox while Anne Mulcahy was CEO. It is an excellent illustration of strategic responses and strategy execution.

In 2000, Xerox was on the verge of bankruptcy. Its revenues were declining, its sales force unraveling and its new-product pipelines depleted. The company had $18 billion in debt, and all lines of credit were exhausted. The share price was in free fall. Customers were dissatisfied and defecting. Employee morale was low and turnover high. It had just one week's cash on hand and key advisers were recommending that the company consider bankruptcy. To make matters worse, the chief financial officer was preoccupied with an SEC investigation into the company's revenue recognition practices.

In the midst of this chaos, as Anne was preparing for a business trip to Japan, chairman Paul Allaire came to her office and told her he planned to recommend that the Xerox board terminate its then-CEO and promote her to president and eventually CEO.

In her new position, she met personally with the top 100 executives to ask them if they would stay with the company despite the challenges ahead…98 committed to stay. The company sold $2.5 billion of non-core assets, exited the ink jet business and focused on business excellence.

In spite of the pressures and endless rounds of meetings at headquarters, Anne rode with salespeople to get into customers' offices. She learned that customers wanted Xerox to help them cut costs. In other words, they wanted business solutions, not just hardware; they wanted low-cost solutions which meant they might buy from a Xerox competitor, and they wanted software and hardware that would help with document-intensive jobs like customized bank statements. To respond, Xerox launched its global services group in 2002. This required a radical redesign of the sales force's work.

Before the change, the sales process went something like this: A sales rep would visit a customer, look for copiers, determine how old they were and sell a new one. The process was predictable, comfortable and unprofitable. Under the new strategy, the salespeople had to become consultants able to engage with customers, understand the complexities of their businesses and find opportunities to sell document management solutions that would solve business problems. The sales process now took longer and the rep had to have a broader business perspective. Not surprisingly, many were concerned about the change. They'd say, "I know how to sell and make a living the old way, but not the new way."

In addition to a radical change of the sales process, Xerox turned a critical eye on its processes for inventory management. Over time, inventory costs were drastically reduced and inventory turns increased. Xerox also tightened its process for collecting receivables (AR days). Overall, the organization was able to eliminate $2 billion in costs within two years.

Xerox bought Global Imaging Systems for $1.5 billion to increase access to small- and mid-size business customers. The acquisition immediately boosted revenue growth. Sales climbed 12% in the third quarter of 2007, compared with a 1.2% increase for all of 2006. Anne expanded Xerox's business beyond traditional copiers and printers into the document management space — contributing $3.5 billion of revenue in less than seven years.

Anne's strategy for Xerox staved off bankruptcy by cutting billions in operating expenses without cutting field sales or R&D. Despite recommendations from various consultants that cutting investment in R&D would generate immediate cash and profit, Xerox continued R&D and engineering investment at the same rate as before the crash. By launching 100 new products in just the last few years with new color and digital technology, Xerox restored profit growth and added revenue streams — though revenue growth has been elusive.

About Xerox's difficult past, Anne shares this lesson, *"The skill is to stay connected to customers and to move quickly to capture the opportunity or avoid a risk."*

Here are the three things I hope you realized as you read this case:

1. Xerox was inside of the "red zone of failure" when Anne took the helm. She needed a strategy that would both correct that problem (short term) *and* position Xerox for a viable future (long term). By continuing to invest in R&D while addressing cash and return-oriented outcomes, the strategy focused on both.

2. Each of Xerox's major strategic initiatives can be mapped to the four business outcomes that we've already discussed:
    CASH
    •   Improved inventory management and turns
    •   Decreased AR days
    GROWTH
    •   Launched new products
    •   Launched global services group/document management business

- Acquired Global Imaging Systems
- Maintained R&D investment

RETURN
- Cut billions in operating expenses
- Sold non-core assets
- Added revenue streams

CUSTOMER
- Tightened relationships with customers
- Met customer needs for business support services
- Transformed the sales process

3. The major drivers for growth came from a renewed understanding of the needs of the customer. No matter your position, take every opportunity you can to develop a deep understanding of your customers and consumers.

Strategic Acumen @ Every Level

There are so many women who've taken the helm of struggling organizations that I've dubbed them "Hail Mary Heroines." In addition to those mentioned earlier, others include Julia Stewart, who as CEO of IHOP turned the struggling franchise into the #1 chain in the family dining sector. In 2007, IHOP bought Applebee's, giving Julia another turnaround in a very difficult economy. Debra Cafaro took over as CEO of Ventas, Inc., in 1999 when the provider of nursing home and other health-care facilities was insolvent. By 2004, it was one of the hottest companies in the industry. Mary Sammons became president of Rite Aid when the company was verging on bankruptcy, its stock price had plummeted from $50 to $1.75 and its former executives were brought up on federal charges of conspiracy to defraud. And we don't know what Carol Bartz will accomplish as she's taken over struggling Yahoo! following a shareholder revolt that removed Jerry Yang from the helm.

These women vividly illustrate that CEOs face strategic challenges...but not CEOs alone — every woman aspiring to lead at whatever level in the organization must enhance her strategic acumen.

In *Know How,* Ram Charan says this another way, *"It isn't necessary that you be a CEO to seek the big picture. While CEOs and business unit leaders need to see the external patterns to position the business, other leaders need this know-how, too, for instance, for HR to do talent planning, for operations to choose plant locations, and for R&D to find new sources of innovation."*

Strategic acumen differs by level and it's never too early to begin to cultivate and demonstrate it. Smart executives encourage strategic recommendations from all levels. Google is famous for encouraging all employees to innovate to stimulate growth. At 3M, employees are expected to devote a percentage of their time to innovation. So, learning to think strategically can begin the moment you put a foot in the door. And the higher you go, the more you're being paid to set, execute and deliver on strategy.

Strategic acumen begins with an understanding of what strategy is, why companies set strategy and the relationship between strategy and financial and other outcomes. Beyond that it means being able to make smart choices about changes that will position the organization for the future. Remember, you can hone your strategic acumen at any level — and if you do, you increase your chances for a no-ceiling career.

► Lead ON!

Would you like to learn more about strategy and strategic acumen — particularly to better understand and monitor external forces? You'll find in-depth supplemental content and exercises at: *www.NoCeilingNoWalls.com.*

Build Strategic Acumen @ Every Level

If you're at **career-start:** Learn how your job fits into the larger whole. Why is your job important in the context of your organization's strategic initiatives? Not sure what your organization's strategy is? Here are several ways to find out. Ask a co-worker or mentor at a higher level. Keep your ears open for organizational changes (e.g. reorganizations, new initiatives, new products/services, moves into new markets) and ask how they support strategic goals and ask about the market forces behind them. Set up a Google alert for your company and pay attention to what news releases are being sent to the press.

As you move up into **supervisory and management** positions, it becomes more important for you to access and tune into key outcomes and organizational capabilities. At the same time, if you're smart, you're developing networks and other resources that plug you into the external environment. Answer this: What innovations have you been able to or could you introduce to support key strategic initiatives? What external relationships are you cultivating to stay informed about trends in your profession or industry?

At the **senior management level,** if you aren't recommending strategic initiatives, you probably aren't doing your job. As a matter of fact, one successful COO prescribes that at this level, 80% of your activity should be strategic and only 20% operational. What threats and opportunities do you see in the external business environment and what strategic initiatives are you recommending to address them? What external relationships are you cultivating to help identify threats and opportunities in the marketplace?

At the **executive level,** you are responsible for external relationships and knowledge that enable you to strategically position the organization for success in its ever-changing business environment. You set strategy and hold managers accountable for execution. What knowledge resources enable you to stay abreast of and tune into what's happening in the external marketplace? How well positioned are you to speak credibly to the external marketplace? How do your strategic initiatives position the organization to avoid the "red zone of failure"? How well do you see and seize opportunities to win the customer preference, create a sustainable competitive advantage and leave money on the table?

As a **board member,** you're expected to help the CEO and executive team look at the organization from 30,000 feet in order to: balance short- and long-term performance; to ensure that their strategy positions the organization for the future and that external threats or opportunities are being addressed in a timely manner; to ensure that the company has the resources and capabilities to execute on its strategy and that the company has developed a workable plan for strategy execution. If you aren't comfortable with your base of knowledge and how it can support these expectations, take action to expand it — most likely through your network of successful executives and seasoned directors.

Strategy Mapping Exercise

Being able to map your activities/initiatives and key outcomes to strategic goals is an important exercise in building strategic acumen wherever you are in the organization.

If you understand "why" you're doing what you do, you're positioned to speak the language of power in business. To map your contributions, write into Column 1 any of your organization's initiatives that support growth, customers or return/cash. Then in Column 2, identify which of those initiatives you own or how you and your team(s) contribute to them.

1. Strategic Initiatives	2. How I/My Team(s) Contribute
Growth Initiatives, for example: • Product innovation, new products • Merger/acquisition • Expansion into new markets *My Organization's Initiatives*	

1. Strategic Initiatives	2. How I/My Team(s) Contribute
Customer Initiatives, for example: • Product quality and/or safety initiatives (e.g. SixSigma) • Service excellence initiatives • Customer satisfaction initiatives *My Organization's Initiatives*	
Return/Cash Initiatives, for example: • Expense management (supply chain management, off-shoring, layoffs) • Revenue enhancement (revenue cycle management) • Process improvement or efficiency initiatives (e.g. lean manufacturing) • AR Days reduction *My Organization's Initiatives*	

Show Them the Money:
Financial Acumen

"A budget is management strategy reduced to numbers...The Board wants a short story. What's the story that the numbers tell? The story behind the numbers is more important than the numbers themselves."

—Fred Macri, EVP
Lifespan

Fred Macri made the statement above while teaching managers and directors how to understand the financial reports presented to their board. His quote gets directly to the heart of financial acumen.

Many say that if you can read a budget or create one, you have financial acumen...or if you can understand financial terms like "operating cash flow margin," or can define the line items in an annual report, you have it. Many finance courses for non-financial managers promulgate this in their approach, and you do need to understand what the numbers are and how they're derived, but that's insufficient. Financial acumen means more than knowing formulas and definitions. **Financial acumen means being able to understand the story that the numbers tell *and* to take appropriate action (strategic and/or tactical) in response to the story.**

Anne Mulcahy needed to learn the story behind Xerox's numbers when she took over as president. She not only faced the profound business challenges you've read about, she also faced a personal challenge — she was lacking in financial acumen. Did that stop her from stepping onto the path to CEO? No. She figured out how to get it. She asked Joe Mancini Jr., director of corporate financial analysis, for assistance. *"He taught her about debt structure, inventory trends and the impact of taxes and currency moves so that she could understand what would generate cash and how each of her decisions would affect the balance sheet."* Anne learned how to use the balance sheet to guide appropriate action to generate cash flow and improve Xerox's overall performance.

It's never too early in your career to develop financial acumen, but at some point, if you don't have it, it could be too late. Not all executives or boards will be as tolerant of gaps in financial acumen as the Xerox board was when it chose Anne. And if you aspire to director positions on corporate boards, financial expertise is increasingly important — especially on the audit committee. To avoid looking like a "deer in the headlights" during financial discussions, develop and hone your financial acumen throughout your career.

You can begin with this brief overview of key financial reports. Once you have a basic understanding of them, you will be able to practice analyzing your organizations' performance and recommend key business actions to positively impact financial performance. Now don't skim this over. WAY too many women I've met could care less about this stuff, but to be an effective leader and move up the organization, you have to understand these four reports and the story they tell, then take action on them!

Income Statement/P&L Statement

This report tells you whether an organization has made or lost money over a time period. Charitable organizations do not always produce an income statement but do produce a similar statement that reports on funding inflow in relation to expenses. Gross revenue is referred to as "top line" and net profit as "bottom line" because of their locations on the income statement.

An income statement could have multiple sections:
- *Operating section:* showing revenue and expenses from the core business.
- *Non-operating section:* revenue and expenses from sources other than the core business — for example, income earned from investments.
- *Irregular items section:* reported separately because the items are unlikely to recur. They would include events such as temporary production stops, effects of natural disasters and changes in accounting principles.

Earnings per share are reported on the face of the income statement. The formula for earnings per share is (net income − preferred stock dividends) ÷ the weighted average of outstanding common stock shares.

Statement of Retained Earnings/Equity Statement

Retained earnings are the portion of net income that a company does not distribute to shareholders but instead holds onto for reinvestment in the business. The statement of retained earnings uses information from the income statement to report changes in retained earnings, which are then reported on the balance sheet as "stockholders equity." The formula is:

$$
\begin{array}{l}
\text{Beginning retained earnings} \\
- \text{Investments} \\
- \text{Dividends paid} \\
\underline{+ \text{Net income}} \\
\text{Ending Retained Earnings (stockholder equity)}
\end{array}
$$

The goal for retained earnings is to have a balance between stockholder equity and market value of the company. If substantial monies are kept for reinvestment, but there is not a corresponding increase in market value, you would be concerned about the effectiveness of the executives' strategy or strategy execution. Similarly, you would be concerned if dividends to shareholders account for a decline in retained earnings over time while there is no increase in market value.

Statement of Financial Position/Balance Sheet

This report is a summary of the organization's assets as of a specific date. Corporate balance sheet account names and usage are country and industry specific. Generally they are reported in two sections:

- **Assets**
  - ○ *Current assets,* such as cash, inventories and accounts receivable.
  - ○ *Long-term assets (fixed assets, non-current assets),* such as plants and equipment or real estate.
- **Liabilities and Equity**
  - ○ *Liabilities,* including accounts payable, promissory notes or corporate bonds. These can be reported as *current* liabilities (owed within one year) and *long-term* liabilities (falling due after more than one year).
  - ○ *Stockholder/Shareholder Equity* is a liability in the sense that it represents funds owed to shareholders after other liabilities are paid.

From the company's balance sheet, you can calculate (or view) three important ratios that are measures of liquidity (the ability to convert assets to cash to meet short-term obligations) and leverage (the ability to meet long-term obligations). These are:

- **Current ratio:** current assets ÷ current liabilities. A good range is 1.5 to 2. If the organization has too little debt (a ratio much higher than 2), it could be undercapitalizing its growth or might be providing inadequate dividends to shareholders.
- **Cash-to-Debt ratio:** (cash + short-term investments) ÷ (short-term debt + long-term debt). A positive value is 1.5 or more. If the organization is carrying too much debt for its size (a ratio lower than 1.5), it is vulnerable — the interest and dividend payments it owes can outstrip its

ability to generate revenue. If it is carrying too little, it might not be using its resources for growth.

- **Debt-to-Equity ratio:** stockholder equity ÷ long-term debt. Companies set targets for this and there is wide variance across industries. Find out what number is considered healthy for your industry.

Cash Flow Statement

This report provides a picture in time of cash into and out of the organization. They are a good indicator of the short-term sustainability of the organization. They complement the income statement or balance sheet in this way — a company might be generating profit but has difficulty remaining solvent. For example, the organization might not have sufficient liquidity to meet its bills if there is a lag between when it delivers its product/service and when it collects payment. (Remember earlier how we discussed the importance of AR days.)

Cash flow statements are broken into three subsets that allow you to analyze the sources of cash and the strength of an organization's core business.

- *Operating cash flow:* also called working capital, is the cash that comes from the core business through sales. The greater the percentage of operating cash to total cash, the stronger the core business.
- *Investing cash flow:* reports on cash generated from sources and uses of cash that aren't related to the core business. Wise investments for long-term return are positive indicators for a company's future.
- *Financing cash flow:* relates to cash from and to external sources (lenders, investors, shareholders).

Wonder why a company might sell receivables, pay employees with stock options, delay payments to suppliers, buy a startup with a proven product and sell stock? These are all ways that a company can augment cash flow.

Financial Metrics

Some of the financial performance metrics you'll see in the reports described above and others are generic. Read, watch or listen to business stories and you'll find metrics such as debt, net income, revenue, earnings, rate of growth, market share and cash used to give evidence of a company's health or lack thereof. Instead of glossing over them, think about *why* they've been chosen and what they tell you about the business. For example:

- When Anne Mulcahy took over at Xerox, stories highlighted seven quarters of loss, $17 billion in *debt* and an *earnings* drop from $63.39 to $4.43 per share. These were signs of a company in grave distress. A story three years later highlighted four straight quarters of operating *profits*, $3 billion in *cash* (up from $154 million) and 21% decrease in *debt,* marking a significant turnaround.
- As a result of spinoffs and restructuring that were part of Kerrii Anderson's turnaround plan for Wendy's, one feature cited the 71% drop in net *income*, a goal of $335 in *earnings*, up from $221. While the smaller company had less income, the overall earnings were up significantly — a signal of a return to health.
- While she was CEO at Burberry, Rose Marie Bravo achieved a 40% jump in *sales*, bringing the company to $1.7 billion in *revenue*. Indicators of robust growth — *if* expenses didn't rise faster than the revenue growth.
- When Angela Braly took over as CEO of WellPoint, the company's *earnings* had increased 55% per year on average and *revenues* had grown 37% per year. That's an astonishing track record.
- Helen Greiner's accomplishments at iRobot were codified by reports of the company's 15 quarters of year-over-year *revenue* growth and record *revenue* of $249.1 million in 2007, up from $189 million in 2006.

- In August 2008, after serving as CEO of TJX for about a year and a half, Carol Meyrowitz's accomplishments were described this way, "But not everything has been burdensome for the 25-year retail vet: Meyrowitz recently reported the company's financial results, including a 4.6% net *income* increase and a 22% dividend hike for shareholders."

In the context of the financial elements of our model for outcomes — cash, growth and return — here are some places to look for performance metrics. (It's assumed that if the financials look good, the customer is being taken care of.) Look for the health of the organization's:

CASH
- Days cash on hand (found on the balance sheet) as a primary indicator in operating cash flow.
- Cash-to-debt ratio.
- Accounts Receivables (fewer is better) found in the statement of financial position.

GROWTH
- Trends in revenue reflected in the income statement/ P&L — you're looking for healthy growth in revenue over time.
- Trends in expenses reflected in the income statement/ P&L — especially if the rate of increase in expenses is greater than or equal to the growth of revenue. This is a danger sign.
- Trends in operating cash flow from a cash flow statement. Increases are indicators of growth, but you also want to see a higher percentage of operating cash flow relative to total cash.

RETURN
- From the income statement/P&L, you're looking for increases in bottom line net profit and increases in earnings per share.

There are financial performance metrics that are company- or industry-specific. For example, hospital boards pay attention to performance metrics such as Net Revenue per Adjusted Patient Day, Medicare Case Mix Indices, Costs per Adjusted Patient Day and FTEs per Adjusted Occupied Bed. These key metrics are important elements of the story about business performance for hospitals but aren't relevant to other organizations. This drives home the point that **to develop financial acumen you have to learn the metrics and stories that are specific to your company and your industry.**

Making the Business Case

In addition to using financial information to read the story behind the numbers and make intelligent business decisions, financial acumen is essential when proposing new initiatives, products, services or capital expenditures. In order to get funding, you can't just say the customer wants it; you have to make the business case for it. In other words, describe the financial benefit that the organization will realize from the new program, product or service. I frequently see this as an area of weakness in non-profit executives and managers. They see the customer/client need but don't make the case for new programs that meet it in a budget neutral or profitable way. Whether you work for-profit or not-for-profit, you can take a lesson in financial acumen from Kristen Montgomery, MS, PT.

Kristen is head of the pediatric rehabilitation service at Hasbro Children's Hospital. She is an example of a manager with strategic acumen — she does a remarkable job keeping up with and considering the business implications of trends/forces in her field.

Not long ago, she and clinical specialist Casey O'Rourke saw the opportunity to develop a constraint therapy program that is only the second in the country of its intensity and protocol. This program could help children regain or enhance the use of arms and hands that have lost functioning due to conditions such as cerebral palsy, stroke or traumatic brain injury. For 21 days, children work in their own homes six hours a day with a therapist. The fully functional side of the body is constrained while they strengthen functioning of the impaired side.

To seize the opportunity, Kristen drew on her financial acumen. She developed a business plan for the new service line. She calculated the costs, developed a pricing model, researched the number of children who would be potential clients for this service, calculated the return that would be realized if the hospital offered the service and presented her proposal to the EVP. As a result, Hasbro now provides this program and is giving children a chance to experience the world with a more balanced use of their upper bodies.

Even if you have a math phobia, it's important to be comfortable with your organization- (or industry-) specific financial reports and the concept and process of creating return on investment analyses. If you're at senior levels, financial acumen is essential for strategy setting and execution. In middle management, understanding the story behind the numbers will help you recommend and take action to improve the business of your business. At lower organizational levels, financial acumen helps you understand actions that your organization is taking. And you can't be an effective member of the board without financial acumen.

Here's an added benefit of stronger financial acumen — you'll be better able to evaluate potential personal investments!

▶ Lead ON!

Tie Strategy to Financials

- Go back to your answers to the strategy questions on pages 92–93. With several preceding quarters of financial information in hand, tie your organization's strategic moves to the financial indicators that drove the move or that were impacted by the move. For example:
  - Did a move into a new market follow a decline in revenue growth? What was the impact of that move on subsequent financials?
  - Was there a major cost-cutting initiative (re-org, outsourcing, sale of unprofitable division) following a

decline in profitability? What was the impact of that initiative on subsequent financials?
- ○ Was an increase in cash on hand followed by an acquisition, stock repurchase or major investment for growth?

Enhance Your Financial Acumen

- Check to see if your company offers a course on financial acumen. If it does, take it. If it doesn't, look for an open enrollment course at a local business college or university.
- Use the information in this chapter to calculate the three important ratios (current ratio, cash-to-debt ratio and debt-to-equity ratio) and find out what the target debt-to-equity ratio is for your organization. Analyze what these are telling you about the organization's current liquidity and leverage position.
- Ask your CFO (or a director with strong financial acumen) to give a financial overview to the members of your organization's internal women's network or affinity group. (If your organization doesn't have one, consider sponsoring one.) If you are a CFO, organize and give a financial overview.

Learn the Story Behind Your Organization's Numbers

- Ask your CFO to review the latest financial reports with you as part of a course you're taking on leadership (i.e. this book!). Again, ask her/him to talk about the story behind the numbers and management actions based on them. I make this suggestion to women who attend my leadership programs. Those who act on it have not only gained tremendous insight to the company, but have also positioned themselves in the eyes of the CFO as someone who is serious about learning the business of the business.

Use the Language of Power

"My mother sent me to law school to learn the language of power."
—Keynote Speaker

As essential as it is to understand the business of business, it is necessary but insufficient. You not only have to *have* business, strategic and financial acumen, you must also be able to *demonstrate* it by using the language of power.

Listening to a keynote speaker say that her mother sent her to law school to learn the language of power, I realized that there is no single language of power. The language of power depends on the realm you're in. The language of law might be the language of power in politics, but **in business, the language of power is the language of outcomes.**

Here's what I mean. Which of these answers, describing how to improve the retail customer experience, is more likely to win the positive attention of the CEO or board of directors?

1. *"We want the experience to be easy, fun, and entertaining, and we want it to make memories…It's important that people have an emotional connection to us."*

2. *"…we have 40,000 to 50,000 visitors a week. Of course, that sort of volume is a great thing, but it also makes it tough to deliver what we promise…Wait times are one of our biggest*

problems... At...our highest-volume U.S. store, we cut the wait time by 40 percent. We are constantly focusing on the inventory situation, from product development to retail...we need to do a better job of steering customers to what's in the store for them."

Chances are the second statement. Why? Because the answer is given in the language of power in business — the language of outcomes. The CEO who's quoted in #2 is talking about a 40% reduction in wait time (CUSTOMER) and increasing inventory turns by steering customers to what's in the store for them (RETURN).

One of my clients told me about a conversation she had with her manager in which he said, *"When I talk with my boss I talk numbers first then people, when I talk with my staff I switch it to people first and then numbers."* She glossed over the comment, but I took her back to it because it was the first time I heard a man explicitly describe using the language of power. What she heard as a passing comment was actually a tremendous gift. Recently, I came across a similar comment made by Hewlett Packard CEO Mark Hurd to Ann Livermore when he first arrived at H-P (where Ann had worked for more than 20 years). To explain his performance expectations, he said, "The numbers tell the story."

Almost any CEO you see interviewed on one of the business shows will demonstrate ease with the language of power. Here are excerpts from an interview with Christina Gold, CEO of Western Union, during which she said WU "[achieved] ***growth*** *of 12% this quarter, very strong growth, international business is up 26%...55% of* ***revenues*** *come from outside U.S....global in 200 countries...Asia has a huge opportunity in the next decade. Money moving around the world is growing at 8%. Western Union is growing our principle faster at 2%... This is all about moving money around the globe to 355,000 locations worldwide...seeing positive growth in 2007 building market share in those corridors. Our strategies are working...***revenue growth*** *of 3% improving month over month."*

And here's what Carol Bartz said on a conference call introducing her as CEO of Yahoo! *"It's no secret that Yahoo! has had challenges over the past year, but as I look around, I see a powerful global brand with a great collection of **assets**, strong technology, good **cash flow** and talented employees."*

If you have mastered business acumen, understand your positional purpose, been cultivating your strategic acumen and have developed financial acumen, you'll want to make sure you're able to use the language of power (outcomes) when you:

Pitch an Idea — As you've already read in Kristen Montgomery's constraint therapy program example, it is essential to be able to pitch an idea by demonstrating its benefit to the company in financial terms and in support of other key business outcomes. Your idea is worth consideration and resources — because it will increase return, improve customer retention, generate growth, improve the cash position, reduce expenses, increase velocity — not because it's a "really cool new product" or a "much-needed" service or a "cutting-edge" program or because employees will like it.

Set Team Expectations — As often as possible, move away from simply telling your team(s) what, when or how. Move away from a singular focus on activities and results. Also tell them the *why* behind your expectations — specifically the outcomes their efforts will deliver. Carly Fiorina gave a great example of this when she was a second-level manager at AT&T. *"So every time we brought new temporaries in, I'd have a meeting and explain to them how their work made a difference. I'd tell them how much money they were helping us save...They needed to understand the value and context of their work if they were to do it with quality."* So, consider adding the "why" when you set team expectations.

Instead of saying...	Consider saying...
We have to complete this project by June 15.	This project is important to our goal of increasing market share to 65%. It will enable us to reach new customers who haven't had the benefit of our product.
We have to reduce the rate of hospital-acquired infections. Wash your hands before touching every patient.	For the first time ever, Medicare's pay-for-performance policy shows the relationship between good nursing practice and revenue. The better the patient care, the higher the revenue. Reducing the rate of hospital-acquired infections through good hand hygiene improves nursing care, keeps our patients healthy and increases income to the hospital. The higher the revenue, the more money is available for equipment, supplies and for investment in your education.

Make a Decision — When making a decision, especially a cross functional decision, it helps to ask what the impact of the decision will be on the customer, cash, growth and return. Here's what I mean.

Working together, the nursing, registration and physician management of an emergency department decided to run a pilot to help shorten the time between when the decision to admit a patient was documented and when the patient was actually ready for admission.

When evaluating the pilot, the commentary was that the unit secretaries in the nursing department didn't like it, the registrars did like it and the physicians were neutral but concerned about one aspect. Instead of becoming a functional turf battle, they shifted the discussion to the pilot's impact on key outcomes: patient safety and quality of care (CUSTOMER), the patient experience (CUSTOMER) and financial results (RETURN).

When they evaluated the pilot through the lens of outcomes, it was a huge success. The new process improved the patient experience, increased patient safety and improved financial results. Instead of considering the pilot a failure, the issues now turned to how to resolve the physician concerns and to fix the problems experienced by the unit secretaries.

Instead of saying...	Consider saying...
I like (or don't like) that suggestion.	That idea is beneficial (or not) because of its impact on [insert outcome].
Let's collect feedback from the team and then decide.	Let's look at the impact on outcomes before we use team reaction to make a decision

Describe Your Accomplishments — It's an uncomfortable time for many of us — that meeting where we have to discuss our performance with our boss. When we have to toot our own horns without sounding like blowhards. And there are other times too when it's important to update key people about our work.

When it's your time for these conversations, instead of focusing on being a hard worker, the number of staff you manage or the activities you do day-to-day, focus on the *outcomes* you and your team(s) have achieved. If you're uncomfortable with self-promotion, remember that when you describe your impact on outcomes, you indicate you're being driven by what the company can do for its stakeholders and customers, not by self-aggrandizement.

Instead of saying...	Consider saying...
I brought the project in three weeks ahead of schedule.	Because I brought the project in three weeks early, we contributed $759K to the bottom line.
We hit our sales goals.	By hitting quarterly sales goals, we contributed to positive cash flow.
I launched the off-site lab.	My lab is bringing in net $200K revenue each month.

Introduce Yourself — We call outcome-focused introductions your "elevator pitch" because you are pitching/explaining why what you do is important to the organization. A few years ago I was watching TV in the morning and tuned into a commercial that went something like this:

An interviewer, standing in the streets of New York, asks random people as they walked by, "What's your job?"

Various men and women give answers like "I'm a lawyer" or "I'm in accounting" or "I'm a programmer."

The last person answers, "I help leading companies achieve their business objectives."

Now, I said to myself, that final answer is a great elevator pitch in action. To put your own elevator pitch in action when you're asked what you do:

Instead of saying...	Consider saying...
I'm an accountant.	I deliver financial information for sound business decisions.
I'm a consultant.	I ensure that a company is executing its strategy and hitting key outcomes.
I'm a nurse.	I deliver safe, high-quality care to patients.

Craft Your Resume — Again, a resume is a place where it's important (even essential) to focus on measurable *outcomes*, in other words, the way you've driven the organization forward. Don't just list the *activities* you've done or the *inputs* you've managed.

Instead of...	Consider...
Team lead for the XYZ project.	Implemented the XYZ system delivering on the projected $XX million in savings.
Answered customer questions.	Contributed to customer retention rate of 98% by providing authoritative and complete answers to questions.
Managed $1.5 billion business unit.	My $1.5 billion business unit grew revenue by 27% year-over-year. Profit growth of ≥15% annually. Market share increased from 15% to 35%.

In business, to speak the language of power is to speak the language of outcomes. Your ability to use the language of outcomes enables you to demonstrate your strategic, business and financial acumen and to enhance the perception of your ability to lead. For women, this is the Missing 33% of the success equation. That's why these chapters are so important…and have been so long.

▶ Lead ON!

CEO-Speak and the Language of Power

BJ's CEO Laura Sen talked about the company at the Oppenheimer 9th Annual Consumer, Gaming, Lodging and Leisure Conference. Portions of what she said appear below. For each statement, check whether her comment focuses on the external environment and/or cash, growth, return and customer.

	External	Cash	Growth	Return	Customer
"Aside from wholesalers and warehouse clubs, our primary competitors are supercenters, specialty retailers and supermarkets."					
"While about 90 percent of BJ's large-format clubs face competition from another wholesale club within 10 miles, we believe there is still plenty of opportunity for growth within our existing markets. And, accordingly, since BJ's clubs already compete with another wholesale club, we are much less likely than our competitors to be affected by major new club competition in the future."					

	External	Cash	Growth	Return	Customer
"BJ's prices average about 20 percent lower than those of supercenters. Our operating costs are significantly lower, the quality of our merchandise is higher and we cater to a higher-income demographic."					
"Supermarkets represent the greatest opportunity for taking market share."					
"BJ's club units run about 20 percent smaller than the average Costco site and 10 percent smaller than a Sam's Club. This strategy allows us a higher density of clubs in each of our markets, which in turn allows us to maximize management support, distribution and marketing expenses."					
"BJ's clubs each carry about 7,200 skus versus Costco and Sam's, which offer about 4,000 to 5,000 stock items per store."					
"In 2008, perishable sales outpaced all other categories, with a 12 percent comp increase. That trend is continuing into 2009."					
"For 2009, the club is focused on improving the quality and presentation of its perishable foods, making investments in some renovations and expanding store count by six to eight units."					

Answers

	External	Cash	Growth	Return	Customer
"Aside from wholesalers and warehouse clubs, our primary competitors are supercenters, specialty retailers and supermarkets."	✓				
"While about 90 percent of BJ's large-format clubs face competition from another wholesale club within 10 miles, we believe there is still plenty of opportunity for growth within our existing markets. And accordingly, since BJ's clubs already compete with another wholesale club, we are much less likely than our competitors to be affected by major new club competition in the future."	✓		✓		
"BJ's prices average about 20 percent lower than those of supercenters. Our operating costs are significantly lower, the quality of our merchandise is higher and we cater to a higher-income demographic."				✓	✓
"Supermarkets represent the greatest opportunity for taking market share."			✓		
"BJ's club units run about 20 percent smaller than the average Costco site and 10 percent smaller than a Sam's Club. This strategy allows us a higher density of clubs in each of our markets, which in turn allows us to maximize management support, distribution and marketing expenses."	✓			✓	

	External	Cash	Growth	Return	Customer
"BJ's clubs each carry about 7,200 skus versus Costco and Sam's, which offer about 4,000 to 5,000 stock items per store."					✓
"In 2008, perishable sales outpaced all other categories, with a 12 percent comp increase. That trend is continuing into 2009."			✓		
"For 2009, the club is focused on improving the quality and presentation of its perishable foods, making investments in some renovations and expanding store count by six to eight units."			✓		✓

Your-Speak and the Language of Power
Where could you better use the Language of Power (Outcomes)?
And what action will you take?

Opportunity	What I Say Now...	How I Can Use the Language of Power to Say it Differently
Pitching an Idea		
Setting Team Expectations		
Describing my Accomplishments		
Introducing Myself		
Crafting my Resume		

Engage the Greatness in Others

The ability to achieve outcomes through the actions of others is central to the concept of leadership. In study after study, women are rated as more effective than men in the area of interpersonal relationships. So, what problem could women possibly have with this one-third of the leadership definition? Is there anything we have to learn about engaging others? Absolutely — there are four important lessons:

- First, we have to be sure we understand the difference between engagement and compliance.
- Second, there are five strategies for engaging others. Women tend to use only three, and for leadership effectiveness, all five are important.
- Third, that it is insufficient to engage others — their efforts have to be aligned to organizational outcomes.
- Fourth, women are rated as being less skilled in building and leveraging strategic relationships.

We'll touch on all four in the following chapters.

Capture Hearts, Minds and Efforts

> "The test of leadership is not to put greatness into humanity but to elicit it, for the greatness is already there."
>
> —JOHN BUCHAN

You may not know about Nobel Peace Prize winner Wangari Maathai. She is the founder of the Green Belt Movement. It began as a way for Kenyan women to counter 90 years of deforestation and, in a way, ended up toppling a dictatorship and ushering democracy into Kenya. How'd she do it? By engaging the greatness in women — many of whom are poor and uneducated. She describes these women as *"persuaded to believe that because they are poor, they lack not only capital, but also knowledge and skills to address their challenges. Instead, they are conditioned to believe that solutions to their problems must come from 'outside.'"*

Through Wangari's leadership, involved women have planted more than 35 million trees to reverse deforestation, address climatic instability and repair soil and water contamination. They stood up against a dictator, police brutality and corruption. And the Green Belt Movement has expanded internationally.

In her Nobel Prize acceptance speech, Maathai, speaking of her followers, said, *"They realize their **hidden potential** and **are empowered*** *to overcome inertia and take action. They come to recognize that they are the primary custodians and beneficiaries of the environment that sustains them…Entire communities also come to understand that while it is necessary to hold their governments accountable, it is equally important that in their own relationships with each other they exemplify the leadership values they wish to see in their own leaders, namely* **justice, integrity and trust***… Through the Green Belt Movement, thousands of ordinary citizens were mobilized and empowered to take action and effect change. They learned* **to overcome fear and a sense of helplessness** *and moved to defend democratic rights. In 2002, the* **courage, resilience, patience and commitment** *of members of the Green Belt Movement, other civil organizations, and the Kenyan public culminated in the peaceful transition to a democratic government and laid the foundation for a more stable society."*

Remembering that this one-third of leadership is about engaging the greatness in others, I'm sure you recognized the portions of her quote that illustrate what that means, e.g. hidden potential, empowered action, justice, integrity, trust, courage, resilience, patience and commitment.

Let's move from the global stage on which this extraordinary woman acts, to explore what it means for *you* to engage and align others. We'll start with what it doesn't mean. Engaging the greatness in others isn't about:

- ○ **Building Dependence** — If people are dependent on you for answers, their greatness remains untapped.
- ○ **Timidity** — If you're timid in asking for greatness, you won't get it.
- ○ **Command & Control** — When you tell people exactly what to do, when and how — you might reap the results of people's efforts, but you haven't captured their hearts and minds. You can't command & control your way to engagement.

- ○ **Carrot & Stick** — You can use the promise of a reward or the threat of a punishment to direct people's efforts, but, again, you haven't captured their hearts and minds.

Engaging the greatness in others means first believing that everyone has greatness in them and then being willing to look for it. It means capturing hearts, minds **and** efforts. In other words:

- ○ **Inspiring** others to care about what they do, the customers they serve and the organization they work for. (Hearts)
- ○ **Challenging** people to think about what they are doing, why they are doing it and how they can do it better. (Minds)
- ○ **Expecting** people to do their best for the customers, the company and their co-workers every day. (Efforts)

Ursula Burns talks about the power of communication and the ways that she and the executive team at Xerox engaged employees and the union in the profound change that was required to turn the company around. They said to them, *"Here's the problem, here's the strategy, here's what you can do to help. You have a choice: You can leave and we'll help you do that or you can roll up your sleeves and help."* This message helped those who stayed engage their hearts, minds and efforts. She says, *"Defections slowed to a trickle, energy returned and our people turned around the company."*

Engagement versus Compliance

The theme of hearts, minds and efforts is important because there's a big difference between engagement and compliance. *Engagement* captures hearts, minds and effort while *compliance* merely drives effort. Let's break this down further:

Engagement	Compliance
Taps into greatness, e.g. skill, attitude, interest, value, vision, sense of greater organizational good.	Taps into dependence, fear, acquisitiveness.
Requires ○ Dialogue ○ Empathy ○ Willingness to Listen ○ Working with Diverse People ○ Developing People ○ Advocating for People ○ Inspiring Confidence **NOTE:** These are behaviors/ attributes on which women are often rated as outperforming men.	**Requires** ○ Incisiveness ○ Directness ○ Decisiveness ○ Expertise ○ Taking Charge ○ Problem Solving **NOTE:** These are behaviors/ attributes on which men are often rated as outperforming women.
Actions Coach Mentor Set Direction Empower Encourage Include Build Team Advocate for Staff Exercise Personal Power	**Actions** Tell Direct Announce Bargain Dictate Explain Threaten Conditionally Praise Exercise Positional Power

Carrot & Stick and Command & Control are the most well-known *compliance* strategies. Command & Control means telling others exactly what to do, when and how. It can be useful in emergencies, when time is very limited or when expertise is lacking. In the long term, continued use of a Command & Control approach creates a dependent and compliant staff.

Carrot & Stick, another *compliance* strategy, means using threats or rewards to get work done. It can be temporarily effective with staff who aren't internally motivated. With them, your challenge is to determine whether they are in the right job for their talents — if not, move them; if so, find a way to engage them. Using Carrot & Stick approaches in the long term creates an entitled, fearful and/or compliant staff.

These compliance strategies help you control people's efforts but don't engage their hearts and minds. So, you can't say they engage people's greatness. This is not to say that they're NEVER appropriate. Sometimes they are — when Jane Metzger, RN, Ph.D and CNO, and Bill Cioffi, Chief of Surgery, took control of the Rhode Island Hospital emergency department the night they cared for 100 patients from the Station Fire (the largest nightclub burn disaster in America's history — 97 people perished), it was a Command & Control environment. Communication went something like this:

> Dr. Cioffi: "Everybody, listen up. I want a nurse, respiratory therapist and a doc at every stretcher in the trauma rooms. You will take direction from two people: Jane and me. Let's go!" *To Jane:* "Jane, get somebody in the urgent area who will keep track of every disaster number and name of patient. I need you to do the same in trauma alley and be tied to me on beds and anything else we will need. Start making sure we have beds available."

> Jane Metzger: "Dawn, I want you down here in the ED. Tell Karen that I want her on the 5th floor so I have constant information on what beds are available and where we can place patients. Dawn, you need to be tied to me managing beds. Tell Karen on the 5th floor to move the 33 patients off the surgical side up to the 8th floor closed unit and begin to make the beds ICU-capable."

There wasn't much opportunity for dialogue and engagement, because the stakes were high and time was limited. Command & Control was absolutely appropriate.

As a woman, it's important to know when to exercise (or describe yourself as exercising), compliance strategies because if you don't, you could be seen as unable to "take charge" and "be decisive." On the other hand, an overuse of compliance strategies will create dependent and entitled attitudes, not engaged and motivated employees.

Seeking Greatness in Others

The most effective leaders look for and identify the greatness in others. It's not always easy to find greatness in people who irritate us in some way, but it's a requirement if you want to be successful in engaging others. Because the goal is to engage creativity, hope, dignity, aspiration, openness and passion (as opposed to fear, hatred, defensiveness, bigotry and violence) the ability to engage greatness in others rests in your heart. Meeting the greatness in others is done without defensiveness or judgment, in other words, with an open heart. Consider how much softer you feel when you encounter a difficult person with the idea, "This person is doing the best that s/he can" instead of with the idea "this person is a jerk." It's much more effective to meet a difficult situation with openness to understanding its every dimension.

Indra Nooyi, CEO of PepsiCo, speaks about the same approach when she says, *"My father was an absolutely wonderful human being. From him I learned to always assume positive intent. Whatever anybody says or does, assume positive intent. You will be amazed at how your whole approach to a person or problem becomes very different. When you assume negative intent, you're angry. If you take away that anger and assume positive intent, you will be amazed. Your emotional quotient goes up because you are no longer almost random in your response. You don't get defensive. You don't scream. You are trying to understand and listen because at your basic core you are saying, 'Maybe they are saying something to me that I'm not hearing.' So 'assume positive intent' has been a huge piece of advice for me."* And this advice has shaped her persona at work. This is why the former PepsiCo CEO described her as "a deeply caring person" who "can relate to people from the boardroom to the front line."

Effective leaders use various skills to seek and engage the greatness in others. These fundamental skills are the same no matter the level you are at. They include respectful listening, soliciting input, a coaching approach, empowering others, and building esprit d'corps within a team. And we know from the chapter on "isn't leadership neutral" that women are seen as outperforming men in related areas, such as developing people and inspiring confidence. For example, among women CEOs, Patricia Woertz of Archer Daniels Midland for her people skills, Kerrii Anderson of Wendy's for her inclusive style and Carly Fiorina for her listening skills.

Meg Whitman, former eBay CEO, has been one of the most noted consensus-builders. Her ability to lead by engaging others derives from her accessible style. She says, *"I like working in groups. I think that one plus one equals four, often if you have the right people in the room. And I like tossing around ideas, coming to a consensus, if we can."*

These engagement skills and others in the chart on page 122 are taught in courses frequently offered by companies. Now we know why. Courses on coaching, team building, communication and empowerment help leaders learn to engage the greatness in others. If you have these skills, you have a great foundation for leadership. If you want to grow in one or more of these areas, you're lucky because many organizations offer these workshops. If yours doesn't, these topics are taught through open-enrollment programs around the country.

▶ Lead ON!

Engagement/Compliance Survey

For a full picture of how your staff views you on engagement and how your boss views you on compliance, go to *www.NoCeilingNoWalls. com* and take the Engagement/Compliance Survey. It gives you a read on which of your engagement skills are strongest in the eyes of your staff and which you can develop. It also gives you a read on the compliance skills that you might want to demonstrate to your boss (though not necessarily to your staff!).

From Compliance to Engagement

Do you find yourself repeatedly in the compliance side with certain people even when the stakes aren't high and time isn't limited? The only person whose behavior you control is you, so set the goal of moving to engagement with him/her by identifying what part of the problem is yours to own. Use the tool below to identify ways of shifting from compliance to engagement.

- With whom do I often use compliance rather than engagement?

- How have I labeled this person and how might these judgments drive my behavior?

- How might my limited engagement skills constrain me?

- What do I like about using Carrot & Stick or Command & Control strategies? (For example, you might feel more knowledgeable, more in control or more powerful.)

- Other factors that motivate me to use Carrot & Stick or Command & Control strategies with this person. (For example, s/he might not know enough to do it alone.)

Based on my answers to these questions, what will I do to use more engagement strategies with this person?

_____

_____

_____

_____

_____

_____

Develop *Your* 5-C Engagement Strategies

> *"I want people who create organizations that get aligned,*
> *get passionate, get really inspired about delivering."*
> —Anne Mulcahy, CEO
> Xerox

Knowing that it's important to engage the hearts, minds and efforts of employees, colleagues, and stakeholders, the question becomes "How do I do that?" How do you catch people's attention? How do you motivate them to leave their comfort zones and step into change? And how do you telegraph their next moves? Stay with me for a minute while I describe what I've learned about this by working with horses.

Horses are herd animals, and to work effectively with them, whether from the ground or from the saddle, I have to become the "lead mare." Every ride is a lesson in leadership. This means many things, but relevant to this chapter, it means that the horse has to be "hooked up" with me. I work on this with my mare when I dismount, secure her reins and walk her in patterns across a 20-acre meadow. She follows me without bolting away or stopping to eat. Aside from my body language, I have no contact with her — neither lead line nor reins in my hands.

This works because I know how to get and keep her attention, I telegraph my moves so she's not surprised and she's confident that I won't mislead her. When she's doing what I've asked, I leave her alone. If she missteps, I guide her back to what's expected. Sound familiar? These are some of the descriptors of effective strategic communication and are at the heart of what I call the 5-C engagement strategies:

- Charismatic visionary
- Compelling leveler
- Champion
- Connector
- Conductor

We've already explained that leadership isn't about maintaining the status quo or delivering the inevitable. Leadership is about change all the time. Reaching for ever more ambitious outcomes ensures that this is the case. That's why great leaders **use the 5-C Engagement Strategies to invite others to step out of their comfort zones and into change.**

Charismatic Visionary

The Charismatic Visionary strategy engages greatness through a passionate belief in a future vision — especially a vision of the world as it is impacted by the company's product or service. In a sentence, people will step into change because you've convincingly said, "Imagine..." and then, "Follow me" and they buy your end point.

If you're like 90% of the women we've studied, you might be wondering, "If I'm not a charismatic visionary, can I still be a great leader?"

Well, based on the business press, certain celebrity CEOs, leadership gurus and many classic definitions of leadership, the answer is a resounding "NO." And it's not surprising because at the end of the 20th century, when the concept of the charismatic visionary was ascendant along with the birth of internet companies, CEOs pitching their new company to venture capitalists had to have a passionate belief in their vision for the company and the ability to convince people to put money behind it.

But the more accurate answer to the question is an unequivocal, "YES, you can be a great leader without using a charismatic visionary strategy!" Why? Because research has shown that those who use this approach with followers aren't correlated with sustained organizational success. As Rakesh Khurana writes in *Searching for a Corporate Savior*, *"…the vision of a charismatic leader is a poor organizing principle for contemporary firms, which increasingly depend for their success on the sharing of intelligence and the dispersal of decision-making authority across all levels of the organization."* And thinking that all great leaders use the charismatic visionary engagement strategy does an injustice to millions of American businessmen and women who use other strategies to achieve extraordinary outcomes for their organizations — especially by dispersing decision-making across all levels.

Compelling Leveler

A leader using the Compelling Leveler strategy inspires extraordinary results by delivering the message that "we're all in this together." A stellar example of a leader using this strategy is the former CEO of a large financial institution. His we're-all-in-this-together strategy was woven throughout his organization, from its team-managed fund structure to its steps to ride out earlier tough economic times — beginning with steep executive compensation cuts. He considered this team focus central to his company's success, *"While we're outwardly competitive, our internal collaboration makes the environment here very dynamic."*

Champion

A leader using the Champion strategy enables the outstanding performance of others by championing their skills and abilities, supporting their efforts and sweeping obstacles out of the way. The Champion strategy was successfully used by an insurance industry VP who achieved extraordinary results and innovation, not by inspiring those who worked for him with a compelling vision of a world made better through automation, but by unleashing their creativity and motivation. He believed in what they could accomplish and removed obstacles from their path. His vision and leadership ultimately transformed the entire way claims were paid, cut expenses dramatically and made substantial contributions to year-over-year return.

Connector

Leaders using the Connector strategy "wire the joint" or use "grass-roots organizing" to achieve or enable results. They engage a vast network of key influencers at every level and in every function of the organization and outside. This strategy is often used by leaders in parts of the organization that set policy and processes for others. A senior executive at IBM used the Connector strategy to change the compensation structure for her specialized population. Faced with doubters (including the HR department), she prevailed, creating new compensation structures company-wide. How? She engaged a global network of others in the company who would benefit from a compensation structure that better fit the business' new strategy and marketplace.

Conductor

The Conductor strategy involves orchestrating structure, timing, boundaries, goals and milestones in a way that creates clear pathways toward desired results. When using the Conductor strategy, a leader, like a great maestro, identifies the way forward, ensuring that the organization is structured properly, has the needed communication channels, and is measuring the right stuff. In many ways, the humble executives who spun the flywheel in Jim Collins' *Good to Great* companies used this strategy.

Pros and Cons

Each of the 5-C engagement strategies has its strengths and weaknesses. And each, when used at its best, creates an invitation for people to leave their comfort zone and step into change.

Engagement Strategy	At its best:	Watch out for:	Motivates steps into change by...
Charismatic Visionary	Engages greatness by a compelling vision, sustained focus and charisma. "Follow me!"	One head, many hands syndrome. Becoming the problem because people won't tell you the emperor has no clothes.	Providing people with a future vision, a picture of what they're moving toward.
Compelling Leveler	Engages greatness by generating a passionate esprit d' corps. "We're all in this together."	Being afraid to break out of the group/team to make tough and/or strategic decisions.	Making people feel like they aren't alone as they move into the unknown.
Champion	Engages greatness by unleashing impassioned performance at all levels. "You can do it!"	Being disengaged or having poor ability to discern capability. Either will not result in the required outcomes.	Making people feel confident in their individual ability to move forward.
Connector	Engages greatness by "wiring the joint," building, joining and mobilizing a network of key influencers everywhere. "Here's what I can do for you, here's what I need from you and, by the way, you should talk with…"	Politicking for the sake of it (not for achieving outcomes) or for self-aggrandizement.	Illuminating what's in it for them if they move forward in service of someone else.
Conductor	Engages greatness by showing the way. "Here's how we can get this done."	Micromanaging and/or squelching self-directed work.	Making the immediate path forward visible and clear, even if the end is unclear.

When Anne Mulcahy of Xerox says, *"I get things done by identifying with the people in the company and by trusting them. I care most about building a good team to lead the company,"* she is illustrating the Compelling Leveler strategy.

When Carly Fiorina writes, *"Believing in someone else, so they can believe in themselves, is a small but hugely significant act of leadership,"* she is articulating the beliefs of someone comfortable with the Champion strategy.

By describing Angela Braly in this way, *"She knows how to build coalitions around her,"* the author is describing her use of the Connector strategy.

And when Ursula Burns states, *"Employees especially need to know what they are signing up for in a journey...Have a vision and make it simple,"* she is describing the need for the Charismatic Visionary strategy.

These are not personality types! Each of the 5Cs is an engagement strategy that can be consciously chosen — and the ability to use each can be learned. None is inherently better than any other because the ultimate effectiveness of an engagement strategy is based on its resonance with the audience. Therefore, when used in combination, they are very powerful.

When talking about the Xerox turnaround, Ursula Burns gave a great example of this. She said that being clear and *counting on people's intelligence* was one of the most important things they did when going through the changes (Champion). They also used a *futuristic business news article* to communicate where they want to end up (Charismatic Visionary). The executive team gave employees a *path forward* (Conductor) and they wanted employees to be part of the path. *"We needed our employees to **engage with us** to...design the solution"* (Compelling Leveler). And, as you already know, they relentlessly *engaged stakeholders — investors* and *customers* (Connector).

Using the 5-C Engagement Strategies

Chances are that you recognize yourself using one or more of the five strategies. Women tend to be most comfortable with and most often use the Champion, Conductor and Compelling Leveler strategies. The Charismatic Visionary is the least frequently used by women (only about 10%), followed by the Connector.

Although successful women might prefer certain engagement strategies, one observation I've made after listening to them is that they are able to shift among them. The higher you are in the organization, the more diverse the needs of your audience — because you are more likely to speak to larger groups of people. That means you have to be able to use all five of the engagement strategies with ease because different "followers" will be hooked by different strategies. Being able to use all five increases your likelihood of engaging all of your listeners and building their confidence in stepping into change.

► Lead ON!

5-C Engagement Strategy Assessment

Which of the 5-C engagement strategies do you use most often? For an idea, go to *www.NoCeilingNoWalls.com* and take the 5-C Engagement Strategy Assessment.

Aligning Your Engagement Strategies with Your Audience

Not everyone responds equally to each of the engagement strategies. If you're not sure you're using the right strategy for your direct reports, teams or others, use the **Action Planning for 5-C Engagement Effectiveness** tool at *www.NoCeilingNoWalls.com*.

Using All of the 5-C Engagement Strategies

Engagement Strategy	How to develop skill in using this engagement strategy.
Charismatic Visionary	• Picture in your own mind the future if the initiative is successful. Use visual words to articulate that future — particularly the benefits to customers. For example, "imagine a world where every patient with XYZ disease can move freely and without pain," *versus* "our goal is to get the ABC drug to market in three years." There's a huge difference between a vision and a goal. • Believe passionately in the future you're working toward. Your passionate belief will be felt as "charisma" by your followers.
Compelling Leveler	• Know enough about the work of others to be credible when you say "we're all in this together." • Develop team-building skills. • Use the language of "we."
Champion	• Develop a very discerning eye for identifying individual strengths. • Articulate the connection between an individual's strengths/skills and the work that needs to be done. • Outline the parameters and turn people loose to deliver on them.
Connector	• Enhance your strategic networking and relationship skills. • Develop the ability to learn the goals of other people and to describe how helping you will help them. • Hone your negotiation skills.
Conductor	• Learn project management skills. • Work with others to create action steps and project milestones. • Use tools to help people remain on track.

Guard Against Overuse

Most of us have one or two preferred engagement strategies, each with strengths and weaknesses. Which are your two most preferred strategies and what do you have to guard against when you use it? (See table on page 131.)

My Preferred Engagement Strategies	What I Have to Guard Against

5-C Engagement Strategy Toolkit

To weave the 5-C Engagement Strategies into your communication, try on these phrases. They're intended as triggers to get you started.

Charismatic Visionary

- Imagine a world where...
- I see a future where...
- You're going to create...
- My dream is that...
- No future is more important than one in which...

Remember, in the best case, these phrases will focus on the benefits to your customers more than to your company.

Compelling Leveler

- By working together, we...
- We have it within us to...
- Collectively our strengths will...
- No team would be better able to...
- As part of the team, I will...

Champion

- I know you can do this because...
- You're sure to succeed because...
- You've been chosen for this because...
- You've done such a great job on XX that you've been selected to...
- Work out the approach and let me know what you plan to do.

Connector

- If you do this for me, here's how it will help you with your project...
- Thanks for taking this on. Now, how can I help you?
- Here's who you should talk with in order to get started. I already paved the way and told them you'd be calling.
- I spoke with ...
- One of your goals is XX, your help with my project/task/activity can help you achieve that goal in this way...

Conductor

- The goal of this project is...
- Let's work together to create the action plan...
- Major milestones that we have to hit are...
- Who's going to do what, by when?
- There are X phases for this project...

Align Others

> *"Personality alone is not what makes a company deliver. It takes insight into how the organization really works and how to link people's actions and decisions to the right priority."*
> —RAM CHARAN
> WHAT THE CEO WANTS YOU TO KNOW

For decades, the skill of engaging others is one where women have consistently been rated as outperforming men. So much so that the tendency of women to lead through collaborative, engaging and inclusive styles, to put the good of the team ahead of any individual, to share credit rather than hog it and to nurture team spirit has been described as *"women's leadership."* I think this is dangerous for women.

If we think that there's a unique "woman's style of leadership," we can blind ourselves to the men around us who know how to engage others. If we focus on engaging others to the exclusion of delivering outcomes, we will create a situation of happy campers on a sinking ship. And if we rest on our laurels because we have interpersonal skills and expect them to move us forward in our careers, we limit our advancement.

Engaging others means more than capturing hearts, minds and efforts. It also means aligning people to key strategic outcomes. As Anne Mulcahy has said, *"I want people who create organizations that get aligned, get passionate, get really inspired about delivering."*

Rowing in the Same Direction

Aligning others means ensuring that employees are working for the best interest of the organization and in alignment with the goals and key outcomes required to keep the organization healthy (strategic goals). **To align others, *you* have to know the outcomes you're leading for or contributing to.** By now you have a good idea of how you impact cash, growth, return and customer. This positions you to support the organization by aligning your and others' actions with its strategy.

CEOs surveyed by the Conference Board have identified strategy *execution* as one of their top three concerns. Assuming a clear strategy, strategy execution becomes an issue when supervisors, managers and executives aren't doing a good job of engaging and aligning their staffs. It doesn't matter where you sit on the organization chart, you can lead for alignment by getting everyone moving in the same direction.

Ursula Burns, CEO of Xerox, makes this point when describing Xerox's turnaround. People often ask her what the secret was…did Xerox have a great strategy or implementation plan? — and they did, but she points out that it didn't have to be perfect. She says, *"If you have great people aligned around a common goal, they can overcome just about any barrier put in front of them."*

To get others moving in the right direction, *you* must have a sustained focus on key outcomes. As a leader (at whatever level), your sustained focus on outcomes enables you to explain *why* a work assignment or project or initiative is important. And this is what aligns people's efforts to organizational goals. With an aligned organization, anything is possible.

Another way to think about creating alignment is to picture a cascade. The external environment drives your organization's strategic goals — its financial targets and other strategic outcome goals (e.g. customer retention rates). These influence the outcomes you have to deliver and the key change initiatives you direct or participate in. These, in turn, shape your leadership actions — where you spend your time, what you communicate, the behaviors you reward and recognize and other messages you use to engage and align your team.

Your leadership actions help others' actions — e.g. if you're a manager this means the actions of your team(s).

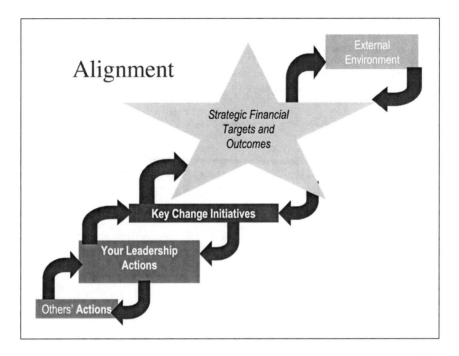

Success means that others' actions reinforce your effective leadership. This results in achievement of the goals that your change initiatives support, the company achieves its strategic and financial outcomes, and its strengthened position in turn has an impact on the business environment.

The message here for you is that you can't slog unconsciously through your daily actions. You'll want to consciously consider each act and each conversation as an opportunity to align others. Think about questions like these:

- If someone observed your actions over the course of a week, would they see your greatest time invested on your most important outcomes?
- If you analyzed your staff meetings, do you spend the most time on key outcomes?

- Based on the topics you've discussed with them, would your staff know which are the most important outcomes they contribute to?

It's a natural tendency to apply effort to tasks that we enjoy. If what you enjoy doing at work isn't directly tied to the key outcomes you are driving, you will have to manage yourself carefully.

Strategic Communication

It's also essential to consider every conversation as an opportunity for strategic communication. **Strategic communication means using consistent and clear messages and appropriate processes, mechanisms, and media to keep an organization focused on achieving or exceeding strategic goals.** It gets people engaged and aligned to achieve extraordinary outcomes. It begins with strategy and ends with messaging. While you might be thinking that strategic communication means grand speeches, annual reports or other singular events, *every* interaction a leader has is an opportunity for strategic communication. To know how well you do at aligning your organization through strategic communication, ask yourself:

- What percentage of my employees can articulate the key outcomes they're supporting?
- How often do I add the *"why"* when I describe the *"what"* that needs to be done?
- When I give feedback, how focused on and aligned with outcomes is it?
- What about rewards — when I feature someone's accomplishments, how closely and explicitly is the reward tied to key outcomes?

Paula Reynolds, CEO of Safeco, illustrates the importance of alignment and strategic communication when she said, *"My big thing is around coherence which is this: If I come in and I say something to you like, 'Today we're going to only sell homeowners polices' and then by 3 in the afternoon I say to Mike, 'We're going to sell car policies today' and then*

I go to Laurie and say to her, 'We need to run some media stuff that says we've got surety polices for sale today,' everyone will have the sense that it's not coherent…When you're a CEO, anything you do in that regard is magnified through the [organization]. As a CEO, you have to have a game plan that will hang together…You have to build this coherent framework where everything you're doing hangs to some central principles."

To illustrate how you can power up your strategic communication by weaving outcomes into what you say and paying attention to the engagement strategy you use, let's look at three examples.

Instead of this...	Say this...
Luluah, your project management skills are outstanding and that's why you've been chosen to lead the project team. I know you can get it done.	Luluah, our **customer service strategy** rests on completing the call center project on or ahead of schedule. Your project management skills are outstanding and that's why you've been chosen to lead the project team. I know you can get it done. *This example uses the Champion engagement strategy to connect Luluah's actions to a CUSTOMER-focused outcome.*
Tonia, the team needs to hear your ideas. What are your thoughts on how to **improve productivity?**	Tonia, you have an incredible ability to see creative solutions. The team needs to hear your ideas. What are your thoughts on how to **improve productivity?** *A Compelling Leveler request focused on RETURN.*
Pat, that was a great suggestion. Thanks.	Pat, that suggestion is exactly the kind of solution-oriented proposal that helps us stay on track and opening in Asia on schedule. Thanks. *Positive feedback focused on GROWTH.*

Building a coherent message is something that you can do no matter where you are in the organization. You can (and should) begin long before you make it to the CEO's office! Be relentlessly focused on outcomes in what you do and what you say. Know the outcomes you're driving, prioritize your time based on the outcomes, use communication to help others stay focused on key outcomes and be consistent in what you emphasize and reward.

▶ Lead ON!

Alignment @ Every Level

At every organizational level, there are actions you can take to lead for outcomes by supporting organizational alignment. The actions are additive, so take a minute to read through them all.

Alignment actions at the **individual contributor** level:
- Keep your focus on your individual goals to make sure you're hitting targets.
- Prioritize your time on the basis of activities that are most important for delivering key outcomes.
- Through your example and discussions, be a role model to your colleagues.

At various **management** levels, make sure you keep yourself focused on key outcomes and maintain the right focus for the individuals/ teams that report to you by:
- Posting team and individual metrics that relate to key outcomes (you can post individual metrics anonymously by assigning numbers to individuals. One team significantly improved a number of safety and quality metrics by showing each member how her/his performance compared with her/his peers).
- Discussing progress on outcomes in team meetings.
- Organizing your meeting agendas around key outcomes.
- Helping teams remain focused on overcoming any roadblocks to goal achievement.

- On a daily basis:
  - Link praise and rewards to outcome achievement and be public with praise.
  - Coach performance in the context of key outcomes — do this in private.

At the **senior management/executive** level, you do all of the above and support alignment by:
- Developing the strategic communication skills of your managers through observation and coaching.
- Ensuring that formal strategic communication (e.g. newsletters, updates, management forums, etc.) sustain a focus on key outcomes.
- Finding ways to align large groups of employees by engaging their greatness as if you were speaking to each individually.
- Guarding against "flavor-of-the-month" initiatives and messages.

For a more in-depth **Alignment @ Every Level Assessment** tool, visit *www.NoCeilingNoWalls.com.*

Power Up Your Strategic Communication
Here's a chance for you to power up your strategic communication for alignment. Answer the following:

1. The key outcomes I need to keep in mind for all formal and informal communication are:

2. I could better align my staff meetings to outcomes by...

3. A person I need to praise in the context of outcomes is
   _____. What I should say to him/her is...

4. A person I need to coach in the context of outcomes would
   be _____. What I could say to her/him is...

5. A way I could make our impact on outcomes more visible
   to everyone would be to...

Build Strategic Relationships

"By working so hard to get great results, [women] often take away time from building critical business alliances...Given the opportunity to stay in their offices and make sure their report is perfect or going out of their office and talking to Joe about his business, women are more likely to do their own work."
—VIVIAN EYRE, MANAGEMENT CONSULTANT

So far we've primarily focused on engaging and aligning direct reports, but leadership success also requires that you engage and align others inside and outside the organization: bosses, peers, colleagues, customers and consumers, providers, potential alliance partners, regulators, legislators and other stakeholders. That's why this chapter focuses on engaging the "right" others.

Another way of saying this is **effective leaders have strong strategic networks.** And while we are seen as having exceptionally strong interpersonal skills, **women are perceived as not having strong strategic networks.** For example, we are rated as underperforming men in three areas: being able to build alliances, having many contacts and being sophisticated about organizational dynamics.

The Value of Strategic Networks

It's never too early (or too late) in your career to begin to develop your web of strategic contacts. What makes these relationships different from casual contacts or friends is that *strategic* contacts are or could be people who can help you meet your business and personal goals — whether they are connected with your current position or goals for your future. A relationship is not strategic if you don't have a goal. So, to make your *net* work, hold your goals in mind.

Why is this important? Because people generally want to help others achieve what's important to them. Think about it, aren't you generally willing to help out when someone asks you for help with something truly important? Probably. You might not always be in a position to help, but if you are, you'll most likely offer. The same is true when you ask others for assistance with *your* goals. Most will want to give you a hand — most people have a generous spirit.

Generosity must be a two-way street. This is something I call *explicit reciprocity*. Here's how it works. If someone helps you, for example, by providing information, guidance or a contact, you must be willing to return the favor. You do this by directly offering future assistance to her/him, "You've been so helpful, if there's anything I can do for you, please be sure to let me know."

At the same time, when you help someone, don't be afraid to set up the conditions for future help from her or him if it's not offered. Respond to a "thank you" with something like, "You're welcome. I'll be sure to be in touch if I need assistance from you."

One challenge for many women is viewing relationships from an either/or perspective. We think, either this person is my dearest, bosom buddy (in which case we cement our strong bond by spending lots of time with her) or she is not (and we don't have to think about her again). Unfortunately, this causes women to hold each other to a tough standard. If a woman is in touch only once in a while for assistance, we might feel "taken advantage of," instead of appreciating that she's a member of our web of contacts. This feeling is exacerbated if we don't feel comfortable reaching back to her with a request for assistance. This is a great opportunity to radically reframe our thinking.

One radical reframe is to cultivate what sociologist Mark Granovetter describes as the "weak tie" — a casual, but friendly social connection. This is something that men do with great skill and comfort. With a weak tie, you can feel free to be in touch as the person comes to mind — which might be once a year or even less frequently. Expect and be open to using and being used as a "weak tie" resource.

Another way to reframe is to remember that strategic networks are about both *giving* AND *getting*. There are so many ways today to give to people with whom we have weak ties. Forwarding articles of interest, leaving a voice mail congratulations for a promotion you've read about in the local business press or LinkedIn update or making an immediate phone or e-mail introduction are all ways to be generous to those in our strategic network. Nurture the "strong bonds" and "weak ties" in your strategic network by keeping in touch, sharing important information, sending congratulations, praise and gratitude.

Internal Strategic Networks

Everyone you work with has the potential to become a member of your strategic network. By definition, you have the opportunity to help them achieve their goals and they, yours. But, you have to take time to develop relationships if this is going to happen. And many women, like Billie Williamson, Americas Director of Flexibility and Gender Equity Strategy at Ernst & Young, find this a hard thing to do. She says, "...*[I was] very focused on going through the to-do list, and finishing the job. Then I wanted to go home and take care of my child and family. So I didn't invest enough time in building relationships with people at different levels. I do that today, but I wish I'd known to do it earlier.*"

So, how can you be smarter about investing time building strategic relationships at work? First, treat everyone with respect and be open about how each of you can help the other. Beyond that, picture who's in your personal "value stream." Your personal value stream is comprised of the people who make your work possible because they provide materials or information and the people whose work you make possible the same way. For example, if you're in the sales department, people in your "value stream" might include marketing (for lead generation) and customer service for onboarding and serving the new clients you bring on. It's essential that you have good working relationships with them. And it should go without saying that you will want to sustain good working relationships with your direct reports (if you have them), your boss and others in your reporting chain.

Another helpful internal resource can be your internal women's network. Participation in such a network is built around the idea of reciprocity: members will be willing to help other members. One example of a woman who has used her network with incredible success is Peg (not her real name). Peg not only has taken leadership positions in the network — a step that gave her positive visibility — she also used the network to vet a possible career move. Being considered for what she thought might be a "plum" job, she reached out to network members to provide information about the function, the hiring manager and the position. Several had good relationships with the hiring manager and offered to speak on her behalf. Others provided a window into the position that she needed in order to make a smart decision.

Like Peg, the women we've surveyed use internal networks (whether organic or women's) in a variety of ways. When asked to choose the top three groups out of 14 possibilities, 63.6% of women use colleagues as contacts for career success, and 36.4% use people at higher levels. In order to obtain information about internal open positions, more than 70% use colleagues and 90.9% use people at higher levels. To obtain guidance about career and professional development, 73% talk with colleagues and 46% with people higher than they. And for building a reputation as a competent, credible professional, 64% use colleagues and 45% draw on people at higher levels.

External Strategic Networks

Your internal network will be easier to cultivate than your external, but both are important. Paula Reynolds, CEO of Safeco, makes this point, *"I think that you have to be externally focused at all times as a leader, that is a leadership imperative. Sometimes women leaders are internally focused supporting the institution. Women leaders who make it all the way to the CEO level come from positions that have had more external focus and connectedness."*

And the women in our survey made the point as well. When looking for information about open positions outside their companies, 63.6% use people they've met through professional, industry or trade organizations. They rely on these people also for guidance on career or professional development (46%). And online professional networks (e.g. LinkedIn) factor in as resources for enhancing their reputations (46%).

When you think about career moves, think about those that offer the opportunity to develop external strategic relationships. The higher you are, the more important this becomes. And, no matter where you are, when thinking about engaging and aligning others, be sure you focus on your larger network. Let's revisit Anne Mulcahy's story. What were among the first things she did? Sure, she met with her top 100 managers. But she also went with sales people on customer visits. And she reached out to Warren Buffet for guidance. Each of those was a step to engage and align others.

And remember Mary Sammons, CEO of Rite Aid. When she had no cash available to implement her operating plan, what did she do? She learned about the Rite Aid customer base by developing an internal network of associates in the stores and distribution centers. She also spent time with suppliers. Neither cost money and both later helped her execute her strategy when the financial picture improved.

So, how can you think about the world outside of work and the opportunities it presents for strategic relationships? Consider becoming active in local or national industry or professional organizations. What professional, trade, industry or women's organizations can help you meet people who can help you stay in touch with trends, issues and opportunities? Think about organizations that exist in your external marketplace (especially those that have a strong influence on your organization's strategy) and get to know people who work in those organizations. Identify organizations (professional, not-for-profit, community) outside of yours to which you'd like to contribute. And think about other venues where additional exposure (speeches, articles, white papers) could help your business or your career.

Networking Mentors

You might know Mireille Guiliano as the author of the bestseller, *French Women Don't Get Fat*, but she was also the president and CEO of Clicquot Inc., the American subsidiary of the French champagne house Veuve Clicquot. During her tenure in that position, she guided Veuve Clicquot in America through double-digit growth annually and from startup to 23% market share. Insiders attribute much of her success to her savvy networking skills.

Now, networking about champagne presents some luscious possibilities that networking about widgets might not, but — hey — there's still a lot to learn from Mireille.

> **Be Strategic:** Before she went to Veuve Clicquot, she represented the French champagne industry for a PR firm. There she made connections with key industry insiders by launching a program of champagne dinners and tastings at cooking schools. Later, while at Clicquot, she would tell her employees, *"If a journalist calls for information, that is the priority. If you have to work until 9 o'clock to prepare materials for them, you do it."* As Mireille did, you need to understand who your key stakeholders are, identify and get to know insiders and players in the field or industry that you represent.

> **Get Beyond Golf — Creative Social Events:** Once at Veuve Clicquot, Mireille spread the word about its champagne by word of mouth (pun intended). She held a dozen or more parties each year to feature Veuve Clicquot and spread the word about its quality.

> Creative social events aren't possible only if you represent a champagne company — *PINK* magazine has featured women who take key clients on jaunts to great resorts. Lisa Bergeron, president of Leading Women of Southeastern New England, favors client meetings at area spas.

Nurture Your Network: Mireille explains, *"When I read about a woman in business or the arts achieving an honor, I send a personal letter of congratulations and a bottle of La Grande Dame."* And she adds the woman's name to her database for invitations to consumer events in that city.

At a tasting event, Mireille heard that Mrs. Getty preferred Veuve Clicquot. She immediately sent a bottle with a note. The Getty family made the champagne fashionable among friends and featured it when their children opened a restaurant.

Madeleine Albright, former Secretary of State, was being encouraged to go for the Secretary of State position and voiced her interest to the White House. Many in the Democratic party machine said that she shouldn't campaign for the job, but she was sure that her two male competitors were activating their networks to lobby President Clinton for the position. In her autobiography, *Madam Secretary*, she describes how her network (begun when she was on the board of a private school) helped her attain the position.

"As the non-campaign for secretary began, my own network was small compared to those of [the two leading candidates], but it did include some smart and determined people.... In addition, each day Elaine Shocas sorted through information provided by well-placed allies who gathered intelligence, provided suggestions and put out fires. They had excellent sources and so we were often able to stay a step ahead. For example, we learned that one rival camp was about to tell reporters that a female secretary of state would be unable to work effectively with conservative Arab leaders. We immediately directed reporters to Arab diplomats at the UN, who said the allegation was an insult and gender was not an issue in their diplomacy."

Karin Gilford, VP and general manager of Yahoo! Entertainment, makes a point of networking with other women. At home, she takes women to lunch at her favorite fresh food taqueria, on the road she takes advantage of the opportunity to nurture relationships as well, for example with Lisa Kraynak, SVP of strategic marketing for NBC/Universal.

What can you learn from Mireille, Madeleine and Karin? To develop, nurture and strategically engage a wide network of relationships both inside and outside of your company.

► Lead ON!

Extend Your Network/Map Your Network

Take advantage of additional tools for identifying and extending your strategic networks at *www.NoCeilingNoWalls.com.*

Nurture Your Network

Ask yourself these questions:

- In the recent past, who has helped you with your goals? How have you thanked them? Have you set up conditions of reciprocity by offering your help in the future? If not, do it right now!

- Think about two people in your network whose goals you know. Who or what do you know that might be of assistance to them? What can you offer to proactively help them achieve their goals? Think of contacts, articles, book referrals, or other resources.

Your Internal Women's Network

Does your company have an internal women's network? If it doesn't have one, consider starting one. If it does, get involved! They often provide excellent opportunities for extending your network. You might join as a member, get involved in a committee, offer to take on a leadership role or act as a sponsor.

Use the Greatness in You

Krystal (not her real name), a senior manager in an F100 company, is describing her career history to me. She lights up as she talks about a project she worked on several years ago. As she describes her more recent accomplishments, she speaks with pride, but the light isn't there.

This is an experience I've had repeatedly. I hear women (and men) describe leadership experiences that light them up with joy and others that bring the pride of accomplishment but not the light of joyfulness. Here's why: The more aligned a position is with their personal greatness, the greater the joy.

For Krystal, both positions tap her attributes and strengths, but the earlier position was also more strongly aligned with her values, worldview and personal purpose. This is why she lit up when talking about it. But she wasn't conscious of this.

As a leader, when you are in a place of pride *and* joy — in other words, a place where you can shine — your power to engage the greatness of others is magnified. Why? Because you are fully using the greatness in you — this makes you magnetic. To find your places to shine, heed the call: *Leader, know thyself.*

I find talking about personal greatness a bit difficult, because right off the bat — if you're like many other women — you're probably thinking "greatness? Who, me, great? Nah, that's just too conceited and I'm humble."

But let me assure you. Just as I've asked you to look for and engage the greatness in others, you have greatness in you. Pause a minute and take this in...you have greatness in you...and your greatness is the foundation of your ability to lead! After all, the greatest resource you bring to leadership is who you are!

We have a lot to cover on the concept of personal greatness. So let's dive in and explore how you can use the greatness in you to achieve and sustain extraordinary outcomes by engaging the greatness in others.

Lead from Personal Greatness, Part 1

"If you can't bring your whole self to what you do, you're leaving something on the table — your competitive edge...[Authenticity] is having the courage to know what makes you comfortable in your own skin... People can smell when you're authentic, and they trust you completely when you are — and that's how you lead, with that heartfelt trust."

—SUSAN SOBBOTT, PRESIDENT
OPEN FROM AMERICAN EXPRESS

In the literature on leadership, discussions on **personal greatness include six elements: attributes, strengths, values, worldview, leadership in a whole life context and personal purpose.** I like to present them as a star because, after all, each of us shines!

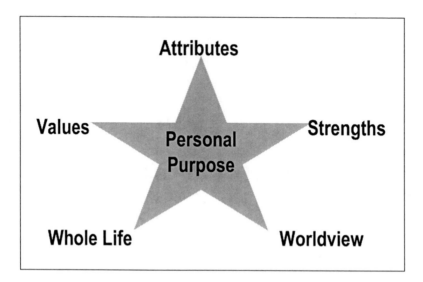

The part of our definition that says, "Leadership is using the greatness in you," means that you are standing on the foundation of personal attributes and strengths, behaving in alignment with your espoused values, conscious of the worldviews you hold (especially your growth mindset) and open to those of others, incorporating your leadership role into your whole life and leading from a sense of your personal purpose.

For now, here's a brief summary of each of the six elements. We'll delve further into each in this chapter and the next.

Element	
Attributes	Personal characteristics or traits — they describe the way you are. Some frequently mentioned as present in leaders include: curious, ethical, daring, passionate, candid, reliable, consistent and authentic.
Strengths	Things you've learned and do well: skills and knowledge, including professional skills, technical skills, interpersonal skills and knowledge you have of your profession, industry, business environment locally, nationally and globally.
Values	The "right and wrong" compass that guides your actions. The issue for leaders is acting in alignment with espoused values.

Worldview	The lens through which you interpret all that happens. This lens is the unique product of your life experiences. It influences how you interpret events, feel about them and act on them.
Whole Life	Your organizational leadership role in the context of your whole life. Literature and successful executives speak about community involvement, balance, being interesting because of outside interests, staying healthy and resilience.
Personal Purpose	Your life's purpose, personal mission, life vision. This might be discovered while thinking about the personal legacy you seek to leave behind. Knowledge of your personal purpose invites an exploration of the alignment between your purpose, the work that you do and how you bring yourself to your work. It is at the center because it influences (and is influenced by) all the others.

Attributes and Strengths

At Leading Women, we differentiate strengths from attributes in this way: attributes describe ways you are. **Your attributes are your inherent traits** — e.g. outgoing or contemplative, curious, compassionate, consistent and/or daring, dramatic, dedicated. **Strengths describe skills you've learned *and* that you do well.** Your strengths include what you've learned about your profession or about executing your role. For example, you could be a superb project manager or excel at leading business development teams; you might be a strong marketing professional or a cutting-edge researcher; a great strategic thinker or excel at board and investor relations.

Take Oprah Winfrey as an example. Most people would describe her as compassionate and charismatic — those are two of her *attributes*. As the CEO of Harpo Entertainment Group and one of the wealthiest women in America, she is also a woman with incredible business acumen — that would be an area of strength.

Recruiter Jeff Christian described one of Carly Fiorina's strengths this way when discussing her candidacy for the CEO position at H-P, *"What struck me was that in her career, she constantly had been sent into troubled situations. And at every juncture except one (a Lucent-Philips*

joint venture to make telephone handsets), she had been able to fix things.
She had a methodology. *She would go into an area and spend a lot of time listening at first."* Carly applied her listening skills as one ingredient of a methodology for uncovering employee solutions to problem situations.

Here are examples of the often widely different attributes and strengths used to describe a number of executive women.

	Is Noted For... Attributes	Strengths
Kerrii Anderson, former CEO, Wendy's	Inclusive	
Carol Bartz, CEO, Yahoo!	Sense of humor	Management skills Ability to cut deals
Angela Braly, CEO, WellPoint	No ego Good listener	Skilled at public policy Ability to court stakeholders
Ursula Burns, CEO, Xerox	Problem solver Direct	
Ho Ching, CEO, Temasek Holdings	Sharp Incisive	
Mireille Giuliano, former CEO, Veuve Clicquot		Master at networking Genius at soft-selling
Daria Hazuda, Scientific Director, Merck	Creative Non-linear thinking	
Mellody Hobson, president, Ariel Capital Management and Ariel Mutual Funds	Fearless Credible	Gift for identifying talent
Sallie Krawcheck, former Chair and CEO, Citi Global Wealth Management	Sense of humor Attention to detail	Strategic thinking

Anne Mulcahy, former CEO, Xerox	Straightforward Hard-working Disciplined	
Indra Nooyi, CEO, PepsiCo	Tough Tenacious Deeply caring	
Barbara Turf, CEO, Crate and Barrel	Humble Fearless	Strong management skills
Meg Whitman, former CEO, eBay	Collaborative Accessible	Consensus-builder
Patricia Woertz, CEO, Archer Daniels Midland	Smart People skills	
Ellen Kullman, CEO, DuPont		Ability to "see around corners," grasp the potential of a business
Lynn Elsenhans, CEO, Sunoco	Smart Decisive	Strong decision-maker

Are the cited strengths and attributes the only ones these executives have? Certainly not. But they are the ones that stand out for those who work with and write about them. Are any of them gifted in the entire list? Most assuredly not. So take heart. You don't have to embody them all to be great. But you do have to know the strengths and attributes that are *your* foundation for leadership.

As a matter of fact, leadership seems to be more about leveraging individual strengths and attributes than becoming cast in the mold of any single other person. British researcher Jane W. Davidson and her colleagues concluded after extensive study, *"The evidence we have surveyed...does not support the [notion that] excelling is a consequence of possessing innate gifts* [i.e. strengths and attributes]."

Successful executives repeatedly say they've learned how to leverage their strengths and surround themselves with people who are smarter and better in their areas of weakness. For example, Kerrii Anderson became interim CEO of Wendy's without having come up through operations. She capitalized on her inclusive style to engage the franchise community and corporate staff in the Wendy's turnaround. She filled a gap in her operational expertise by creating a COO position and filling it with David Near, whose operations experience included owning 29 Wendy's restaurants and serving as president of the Franchise Advisory Council.

Andrea Jung, CEO of Avon, has a strong marketing background, is a strategy expert and constant re-inventor. These serve her well as CEO. At the same time, she speaks about the importance of surrounding yourself with smart people with skills you don't have. *"Spend the time to ask yourself who you can get who can be better than you. Constantly look for new ideas, new eyes, new perspectives."*

The important message about strengths and attributes is to know yours, use them as a part of your foundation for leadership and surround yourself with people who complement them.

Values

Your values are your moral compass. They are the rights and wrongs that ACTUALLY guide your decisions and your behavior. In other words, values finish the statement, "to be a good person, I *must...*" As a leader, your *values* might lead you to:

- Be egalitarian *or* to favor winners
- Show compassion *or* stick to the rules
- Be brutally honest *or* be diplomatic and tactful

Don't confuse values with aspirations. Aspirations finish the statements, "I *want* to be/have..." or "It's important to be..."or "I think well of people who are..." Aspirational statements might include: "I want to be wealthy," "It's important to me to work alone," or "I think well of people who have a strong work ethic." Aspirations are your wishes. Values are your moral compass.

Irene Rosenfeld, CEO of Kraft, has described the golden rule as her moral compass: *"The most important lesson that has guided my leadership and has served me well is the golden rule...it's helped to guide a lot of my managerial actions, it's guided my ability to tell my boss bad news. When you...find yourself in difficult situations when dealing with people, if you apply this screen 'If I were on the other side of that situation, how would I want it to be handled?' it gives you a very clear set of operating principles...I would never ask someone to do something for me that I would not do myself...that has really served me well...as a leader."*

Jane Metzger believes that to be a good person, she must be compassionate, a value she demonstrates with patients and staff alike. While CNO she created a practice where if a nurse didn't pass her board exams, she met with Jane. Why? Because Jane didn't pass her boards the first time. She could be a personal example that failing boards isn't the end of a career. And she used each meeting to offer empathy and encouragement.

While CEO, Meg Whitman wanted eBay to be a company *"with a moral center, a sense of right and wrong."* Her values were tested in two notable instances. Describing how she made the decision about not posting Nazi memorabilia on eBay, she says, *"We are building a brand. We want to be admired and around for generations. And it is the CEO who has to make those judgment calls. So over time, we'd make incremental calls — Nazi memorabilia was one...Ultimately, we said: 'Not a business we're going to be in.'"*

A second test of Meg's values was when she faced a choice between financials and ethics. In 1999, eBay crashed and was down for 22 hours. Sellers stood to lose untold dollars, but Meg decided to not only reimburse sellers whose sale expired during the outage, she reimbursed everyone who had an item for sale. The financial hit was significant, but the goodwill and trust gained paid off for eBay in the long run.

Aung San Suu Kyi is leader of Burma's democracy movement and winner of the Nobel Peace Prize. Two values are at the heart of her leadership — non-violence and action for democracy. Though under house arrest since 1989 and never able to serve as Prime Minister (though she was elected), she has never let fear deter her from action or from pacifism. She's been offered freedom if she leaves the country, but she does not leave. In the face of brutal repression, she continues to stand up for non-violence.

Now I'm not suggesting that you spend your life under house arrest. I am suggesting that to be a credible leader, you must know what your values are and your behaviors MUST give life to your voiced values. For example, if you advocate fairness, but take only certain staff members to lunch, you will have low credibility. To stay anchored by values, consider asking your inner voice, "How proud of myself will I be if I do this?"

As a leader (at whatever level), like Irene Rosenfeld, Jane Metzger, Meg Whitman and Aung San Suu Kyi, you have to know your answers to the statement, "to be a good person, I must..." But that's not enough, you also have to make sure that you align your behaviors with your answers.

Worldview
Your worldview is the lens through which you see and interpret events and the behaviors of others. It is shaped by what you believe and the experiences you've had. For example, Indra Nooyi, CEO of PepsiCo, grew up in India and is a lifelong vegetarian. These experiences shape her leadership as PepsiCo makes major moves into emerging markets and healthy snacks. She says, *"I grew up in an emerging market, and I cannot forget that. I have a basic belief that positive nutrition is important in developing markets."* Under her leadership, PepsiCo purchased Tropicana and Quaker Oats in order to move into more healthy products. When PepsiCo aggressively cut costs in 2008, some of the savings were put toward investing in a new nutrition lab.

Lynn Elsenhans, CEO of Sunoco, grew up in the United States. Early in her career, she worked for Shell and was asked to relocate to Singapore to run its Asia/Middle East refining and marketing businesses. She took it because it was an opportunity to touch the future of the industry — the Asian market. There she came face-to-face with the fact that she had an American world-view. She says, *"My Asian colleagues had the potential for being great coaches to me due to their strikingly different perspective...I realized that trying to impose my model of doing things on someone else was only going to frustrate them. It proved far more effective to understand where they were coming from..."*

Some believe that people are basically slackers, but not Laura Sen, CEO of BJ's. She believes that "everybody wants to do a good job." So she makes it her *"business to understand [barriers to getting work done] and put the teams to work on figuring out how to get around the challenges."* These are a few examples of many possible worldviews each shaped by factors, including nationality, religion, gender and economic status. Let's look at two others that you learned about in Chapter 7 — the *fixed* versus the *growth* mindsets. Here's how they influence your ability to lead.

When your worldview rests on the belief that your and others' mental abilities and skills are static, you operate from a fixed mindset. You either have what it takes or you don't. When facing a challenge, you are likely to **think** things like, "Will I succeed or fail?" or "Will I look smart or dumb?" These thoughts can influence you to turn away from a challenge. As a result, you will have less resilience in the face of setbacks and experience less success.

When your worldview includes the belief that mental abilities and skills can be cultivated, that you and others can change and grow, you operate from a growth mindset. When faced with a challenge, you might think, "What can I learn from this?" or "How can I use this to my advantage?" You can see how this belief and these thoughts influence you to take on new challenges and to learn from failure. As a result, you embrace new experiences, are resilient in the face of setbacks and experience greater success.

Anyone with a fixed mindset would turn a stint in prison into a major life setback. Martha Stewart — the diva of beautiful living — did not. While in prison, she met many women who dreamed of starting a business. Drawing on her growth mindset, she was inspired to stretch beyond her usual subjects of food and decor to write a new kind of book, *The Martha Rules* — a book of advice for entrepreneurs.

Ellen Kullman, CEO of DuPont, has a growth mindset that has served her well. Early in her career, her willingness to learn caught the attention of former CEO Charles O. Holliday Jr. Later, while successfully running a $2 billion titanium technologies business, she was asked to launch a unit focused on safety products. Everyone, including her husband, urged her to continue to run the prestigious titanium tech business. Instead, she leapt into the unknown. She says about her decision, *"…I was intrigued, and I figured that if I didn't stretch myself, then I never would…I learned how to create something from nothing."* She built the DuPont Safety and Protection business to $6 billion in revenues — making it the highest-earning segment. During the time she *"had to change the business model three times before we found the right one."* Stepping into a new opportunity, learning and changing — especially building a business from the ground up — is an invaluable career experience and rests on a growth mindset.

"Fire yourself, hire yourself," illustrates the growth mindset that CEO Andrea Jung tapped in 2005. Avon profits were in decline and management guru Ram Charan suggested that if she couldn't turn around the company, she would lose her job. Confronted with potential failure, Andrea tapped her growth mindset to step up to the challenge. Instead of becoming paralyzed by potential failure and entrenched in her past strategies, she examined the challenges with eyes as fresh as if she were new to the company. She cycled into an action/solution mode and launched a successful multi-year restructuring and turnaround plan. And this pattern continues today.

As Carol Dweck writes in *Mindset: The Psychology of Success,* your world-view *"profoundly affects the way you lead your life. It can determine whether you become the person you want to be and whether you accomplish the things you value."* Your world-view also has a profound effect on the way that you lead! As a leader, strive to be in a growth mindset. It's important for your own development *and* because you act as a role model for others.

► Lead ON!

Attributes and Strengths Exercise
With the examples from our women CEOs, identify the attributes on which you draw and for which you're recognized. What **strengths** do you want to cultivate for success in your current job? Looking toward the future, which strengths do you need to develop?

Attributes I have...	Strengths I demonstrate...	Strengths I'd like to develop...
___ Inclusive	___ Management skills	
___ Sense of humor	___ Ability to cut deals (negotiation skills)	
___ No ego		
___ Good listener	___ Skilled at public policy (or other professional skills)	
___ Problem solver		
___ Direct	___ Ability to court stakeholders (forming strong business relationships with those in your "value chain")	
___ Sharp		
___ Incisive		
___ Creative		
___ Non-linear thinking	___ Master at networking (internally and externally)	
___ Fearless		
___ Credible	___ Genius at soft-selling (using your 5-C engagement strategies)	
___ Attention to detail		
___ Straightforward		
___ Hardworking	___ Gift for identifying talent	
___ Disciplined		
___ Tough	___ Strategic thinking	
___ Tenacious	___ Consensus builder	
___ Deeply caring	___ Strong decision-maker	
___ Humble		
___ Collaborative	___ Ability to "see around corners," grasp the potential of a business	
___ Smart		
___ Decisive	___ People skills	
___ Accessible	___ Other	
___ Other		

Values Exercise

Below is a list of values prompts. Without too much analysis, select the five most important that guide your most moral compass (or add your own).

To be a good person I must...or I must be...		
Accepting	Fair	Practical
Adventurous	Fit	Preserve
Ambitious	Flexible	Private
Authentic	Funny	Productive
Beautiful	Goal-oriented	Prosperous
Capitalist	Hard-working	Pure
Caring	Have integrity	Purposeful
Charitable	Helpful	Reliable
Clean	Honest	Religious
Collaborative	Honorable	Resourceful
Committed	Independent	Respectful
Compassionate	Innovative	Responsible
Competent	Introspective	Self-aware
Connected	Just	Serve others
Conservationist	Kind	Smart/Intellectual
Contribute	Life-long learner	Sophisticated
Cooperative	Loving	Spiritual
Courageous	Loyal	Strong
Creative	Nurturing	Successful
Curious	Open	Tolerant
Decisive	Orderly	Traditional
Dedicated	Pacifist	Truthful
Dependable	Patriotic	Unpretentious
Direct	Perfect	Wise
Disciplined	Persistent	Other
Egalitarian	Playful	
Ethical	Powerful	

Now, in the space below, identify how you lead in alignment with those five values or how you could do a better job of leading in alignment with them.

Value	People see me live this value as a leader when I...	I could better lead in alignment with this value by...
1.		
2.		
3.		
4.		
5.		

Worldview Assessment

Take the **Worldview Assessment** at *www.NoCeilingNoWalls.com* to identify how a variety of worldviews shape your actions as a leader and how to more often lead from a growth mindset.

Lead from Personal Greatness, Part 2

"Authenticity is incredibly important [to effective leadership]...
Being self-aware also is important. Understanding the impact
you have on others and being open to feedback."
—Lynn Elsenhans, CEO
Sunoco

Leadership in Your Whole Life Context

When you read "leadership in your whole life context," does it conjure up the concept of work/life balance? If so, you're like many women we work with. You think about how you balance your leadership responsibilities with those to your loved ones and outside interests. This concept of work/life balance has been foisted on women since the 1970s (I know, I was around when it first came into common usage).

The notion of work/life balance arises from an either/or mindset and is based on the metaphor of a scale. We put work on one side of the scale, life on the other and shape and mold them in an attempt to bring them into balance. Most women I know consider this futile.

Personally, I've found a more useful metaphor in Anne Morrow Lindbergh's notion that *"to be a woman is to have interests and duties, raying out in all directions from the central mother-core, like spokes from the hub of a wheel.*" Instead of trying for balance, I strive to manage my life in a way that I find reward from each spoke and, when possible, eliminate those that offer no joy. Time is limited — the question is not "Is my time equally distributed," it's "How can I get the most joy from the time I invest?" "I have obligations to my family, how can I execute them to give and receive the most love?" Like you, I have to spend eight or more hours at work each day, what choices can I make to get the most enjoyment from those hours?

Woman CEO after woman CEO describes choices made in relation to her interests and duties. Brenda Barnes took time off from corporate executive life to be with her family and sit on corporate boards. Kerrii Anderson, interviewed while she was CEO of Wendy's, said that she married her husband because he made real the possibility of integrating her career and their relationship. They have two children and manage the demands with a nanny and a big Dry Erase board. When Susan Arnold was president of global business units for Proctor & Gamble, she credited part of her business success to having two children and learning to set priorities.

Meg Whitman, former CEO of eBay, has said that during her time as CEO she focused on doing three things as best she could — eBay, being a mom and being a wife. *"There were lots of other things that just didn't get done. We weren't particularly social. We went out on the weekends only when we could bring the kids. I have a lovely home, but it doesn't necessarily look like Martha Stewart just left. I wouldn't say that I'm a fashion forward executive. There was no time. Something had to give."*

So, let something give — and let that be the fantasy of a perfect work/life balance. That being said, there are three additional aspects to leadership in a whole life context that are important to explore: maintaining a healthy lifestyle, giving back to the community and being an interesting person by staying abreast of current events — especially as they relate to your business environment and cultivating outside interests. Let's take them one-by-one.

1. Healthy Lifestyle: The Resilience Factor

No matter the setback or challenge, resilience is what keeps successful women going, and a healthy lifestyle is the foundation for resilience.

It might not be obvious, but many women executives have traveled bumpy roads to the top. Take, for instance, Ann Livermore, who while working at H-P had a kidney transplant. Angela Ahrendts, CEO of Burberry, was wooed away from Donna Karan by Henri Bendel where she was offered the opportunity to open 50 stores throughout the U.S. Eighteen months later, the board stopped the project, giving Ahrendts what she describes as "the most devastating blow in my career." Carly Fiorina was ousted from H-P and bounced back onto the national scene as adviser to presidential candidate John McCain. Carol Bartz received a breast cancer diagnosis on the Sunday after starting at Autodesk on the preceding Friday. In spite of this, she led an amazing turnaround of the company during her tenure. And after years at BJ's, Laura Sen was bypassed for the CEO position and fired by the board due to conflict with the new CEO. She later returned as EVP and then became CEO.

Whether coping with a firing or setback, meeting rigorous deadlines, managing or responding to organizational change or mastering the ongoing demands of executive positions, a healthy lifestyle provides the energy we need to be resilient. Research by Heike Bruch and Sumantra Ghoshal highlights energy as one of two factors contributing to managers' success.

> "After observing scores of managers for many years, we came to the conclusion that managers who take effective action (those who make difficult — even seemingly impossible — things happen) rely on a combination of two traits: focus and energy."

They found that only 10% of the managers they studied had the right combination of focus (on key outcomes) and energy.

We've covered *focus* extensively in our discussion of leading for outcomes. So, what about energy? Healthy living is the foundation for personal energy; we get more than enough advice on this from women's magazines. We are reminded to eat beneficial foods, get sufficient exercise, drink plenty of water, get a good night's sleep, etc. Ways that women who've made it to the top live healthy, replenish their energy and fuel their resilience include:

Mireille Guiliano, president and CEO, Veuve Clicquot	Practices yoga regularly. Walks to work (8 min.). Relaxes by listening to music on her iPod.
Martha Stewart, CEO, Martha Stewart Living Omnimedia	*"I have always believed that having a balanced diet and exercising regularly are of utmost importance. If I didn't eat well, practice yoga and take invigorating walks with my dogs, I'm sure I wouldn't have the energy for my work."*
Kathy O'Brien, marketing director, Dove Skin	Jogs so she can free her mind. Listens to music.
Mellody Hobson, President, Ariel Capital Management and Ariel Mutual Funds	Uses the treadmill for 45 minutes. Does weight training. Recharges by running.
Meg Whitman, former CEO, eBay	Works out every morning.

What do you do to live healthy and replenish your energy in order to be resilient in the face of the challenges of your job?

2. Giving Back

Until the '90s, everyone bought into the interpretation of Darwin's work that gave us a single explanation for evolutionary advancement — "survival of the fittest." Then, at the 1999 World Economic Forum in Davos, Switzerland, Helena Cronin discussed her analysis of Darwin's work. This included her findings about the importance of *altruism* in the evolutionary process. In other words, doing for others is coded into human beings. She told the assembled dignitaries, politicians and CEOs, *"Doing what's immediately good for oneself has been understood by Darwinists for a long time. But what hasn't been understood until recently is that you can actually do better for yourself by being cooperative and altruistic than you can by selfishly refusing to cooperate with others. It's not that you do as well. You actually do better — and all of you do better than if you had gone off on your own and refused to help others."* Among our virtual mentors, we find many examples of altruism and giving back.

Sheila Johnson is co-founder of BET, team president of the WNBA's Washington Mystics, owner of the Washington Capitals and Washington Wizards. She is also CEO of Salamander Hospitality and America's first African-American woman billionaire. Among other philanthropic efforts, she has donated millions to build a performing arts center in her community, to launch the Washington Mystics Foundation to help children build self-respect, self-esteem and more healthy lifestyles, and to support the International Centre for Missing and Exploited Children. As the global ambassador for CARE, she took on the challenge of helping marginalized women around the globe and raised $8 million in 2007 for the *I Am Powerful Challenge*. Within her community, she is active and has said, *"Giving money away is not a transaction, it's transformational."*

Even before they were married, Bill and Melinda Gates discussed the challenge of *"giving wealth back to society in a way that would make a difference."* Their Bill and Melinda Gates Foundation, enriched by a $30 billion pledge from Warren Buffet, funds efforts strategically focused on AIDS, TB, malaria and childhood diseases abroad; and education and homelessness in the States.

In addition to numerous board positions, Susan Ivey, CEO of Reynolds American, serves on the Women's Leadership Initiative for the United Way of America. She is a member of The Business Council, as well as The Committee of 200, an international organization of women CEOs, entrepreneurs and business leaders who provide mentoring, education and support for aspiring women business leaders.

In a twist on the notion of giving back, Indra Nooyi, CEO of PepsiCo, has said, *"After PepsiCo, I do want to go to Washington. I want to give back."*

Why do I share these examples with you? Because it illustrates that leadership in a whole life context includes giving back. Whether through individual habits, philanthropy and/or donated time, successful executives give back, and you can, too. At Coca-Cola, Ingrid Saunders Jones, SVP of Global Community Relations, recently asked all employees to create individual plans that not only included actions on healthy lifestyles, but also on community contributions and environmental action. You don't have to be at the top of the organization to find opportunities to give back — they are all around you all the time.

3. Be Interesting: Cultivate Outside Interests and Stay Current

Cultivating outside interests is important for your mental and physical health. They are rejuvenating and rewarding — they can help us bring a fresh perspective to a business problem or provide the mental timeouts that birth creative solutions. Our virtual mentors enjoy a variety of outside interests.

Carol Bartz, CEO of Yahoo!, enjoys gardening, tennis, jogging, golf and reading. Melinda Gates, co-founder of The Bill and Melinda Gates Foundation, is a runner, kayaker and climber. Meg Whitman, former CEO of eBay, spends time fly-fishing, skiing, hiking and horseback riding. Martha Stewart, CEO of Martha Stewart Living Omnimedia, rides, hikes and does yoga. Indra Nooyi, CEO of PepsiCo, loves music. She played lead guitar in an all-female rock band in her hometown of Madras, India. And, she has sung karaoke at PepsiCo corporate gatherings.

But cultivating outside interests goes beyond what you do for fun or rejuvenation. It also means staying up-to-date with what's happening in the world. In other words, be interested so you can be interesting. The women I call "job nuns" — those who are married to their jobs and have no time to do anything outside of work except sleep and prepare for the next workday — are not very interesting. Why would someone want a "job nun" to join a team? They probably wouldn't.

In contrast, consider this story about Patricia Woertz, CEO of Archer Daniels Midland. When Patricia met auto racing legend Mario Andretti, she grilled (pun intended) him with questions about auto racing, engine technology and aerodynamics. "Some things I didn't even know myself," Andretti recalls. Patricia is more interesting (and interested) than most men who meet Andretti and ask typical questions about his scariest moments or the thrill of winning both the Daytona and Indianapolis 500.

Obviously you don't have to be an expert in engine technology or a karaoke singer, but you do need to be able to at least speak credibly about current events — especially those that impact your business. Make time to follow news — especially stories that relate to your company, industry or profession. And make sure that you have personal hobbies or interests that give you something interesting to talk about.

Personal Purpose

At the heart of your greatness lies your personal purpose. Many of us feel that we're on the earth for some larger reason — even if we aren't 100% sure of what it is. The closer you're able to come to clarity about personal purpose, the better. Why? Because **the more closely you can align your leadership role with your personal purpose, the more gratification you'll find at work and in life and the more authentically you'll be able to lead.**

I don't know whether Carol Bartz, CEO of Yahoo!, considers this her personal purpose, but in my mind it would qualify. *Forbes* magazine asked her what she would like to be remembered for. She answered, *"I want to have done things that my family will be proud of. I have a saying: 'The only responsibility we have on this earth is to be good ancestors.' I want them to be proud of me for a couple generations."* It sounds like Carol's sense of personal purpose is to be a good ancestor for future generations.

Indra Nooyi, CEO of PepsiCo, seeks to align her personal purpose (doing good for the world) with her leadership role. Her profile as one of *Time Magazine's* 100 Most Influential People in the World highlights the fact that she is moving PepsiCo toward more healthy products way ahead of her competitors and that she's making healthiness and sustainability part of PepsiCo's mission. She has described her philosophy for leading PepsiCo as, *"bringing together what is good for business with what is good for the world. We want people to look at this company and think it is a model for how to conduct business in the global world."*

It took Susan Desmond-Hellman, Chief of Product Development at Genentech, a while before she found her purpose. She began her career as a physician working with cancer patients. *"I loved my patients but did not enjoy private practice. I thought it was the wrong job for me. We needed better weapons against cancer and I wanted to be a part of that."* So when Bristol-Myers Squibb (BMS) recruited her husband to work on one of its HIV drugs, Susan went along, joining the company's oncology team to work on the development of Taxol for breast cancer. At BMS, she realized that she had found her true vocation. *"I absolutely loved it! It was a great fit for my skills."*

Finding *your* personal purpose doesn't happen by reading a single short chapter, but the Lead ON! section at the end of this chapter offers some exercises that may help. In addition, think about your career. You have likely been presented with similar exhilarating, gratifying and enlivening experiences over and over. You find yourself passionately responding to certain situations. You find yourself repeatedly drawn to the same life/career dreams. What patterns do you see? In these patterns, you may find clues to your personal purpose.

Once you've identified your personal purpose, ensure that your leadership and your actions are aligned with it. To stay centered in purpose, consider asking your inner voice, "How drawn am I to this situation? Is it a 'should do' or a 'desire' to do?" Likewise, to stay aligned with your highest self, ask yourself, "Is this action based in fear or generosity?"

As a leader, you have a special responsibility to be authentic — to know yourself and lead from knowledge of your personal greatness. So, make your quest for self-awareness a continuous one. Pay attention to the attributes you draw on as a leader, cultivate your strengths, ensure alignment between your espoused values and your actions, understand how your worldviews influence your actions, lead from a whole life context and ground yourself in personal purpose. This is what it means to use the greatness in you! This is what helps you find yourself in a place where you can shine. Nothing is better for an organization. Nothing is better for the people around you. And nothing is better for you!

▶ Lead ON!

Leadership in Your Whole Life

How do you manage your **whole life** in order to feel fulfilled by all aspects — outside of work and inside? What do you do to maintain energy and fuel your resilience? What do you do about giving back to the community? How do you stay informed of current events? Have you taken the advice from the chapter on strategic acumen and begun to read industry or trade news? What personal hobbies or interests do you cultivate? What do you do that gives you something interesting to talk about? Go to *www.NoCeilingNoWalls. com* to answer these and other questions about how you weave leadership into your whole life context.

Personal Purpose: Legacy Exercise

You might get close to a sense of your personal purpose through our Legacy Exercise. Here's how:

1. Take yourself to a quiet place with no interruptions. Imagine that you are about to leave the job you currently hold. You might be moving to a new opportunity or leaving for retirement.

2. On blank pages in a journal, answer the following questions. (For an even more powerful experience, sit with a blank piece of poster board and an abundance of magazines and hold each question as you page through the magazines for images that speak to you of your answer.) When people toast you as part of your going-away party, what do you want them to say?
   ○ What do you want to be remembered for?
   ○ What do you want to have learned?
   ○ What do you want to have taught?
   ○ What other ways do you want to impact the people you work with, for and who work for you?
   ○ What impact do you want to have on the organization?

- ○ What impact do you want to have on your profession?
- ○ What impact do you want to have on the community?
- ○ Who do you want to thank for shaping your leadership? How did s/he/they shape your leadership?

3. Without forcing an immediate answer, hold the question in your mind, "What is my personal purpose?" and see what answers emerge over time.

Aligning Personal Purpose and Leadership

1. Think of your personal purpose and your leadership role as two circles. The more they overlap, the more aligned they are. In the space below, draw your two circles as you experience them today. As you think about how to draw them, consider the following: Are they entirely separate? Do they overlap a little or do they overlap a lot? If they overlap, what expectations and actions belong in the overlap?

2. What actions can you take to more strongly align your personal purpose with your leadership role?

Mine the Power of Language

*"...I had often hesitated to make a point during meetings for fear that
it, and I, would be dismissed as stupid, only to have some man make
the same point — and be considered clever. 'Speak up!'...'Interrupt!'"*

—MADELEINE ALBRIGHT
MADAME SECRETARY

I've had the privilege of being acknowledged as one of "40 Women
We Admire" by Big Sisters of Rhode Island, chosen by *Providence
Business News* as Ally and Mentor for Business Women and honored
along with 22 other women. I share this because of an observation I
made about my 60+ co-honorees. These successful women are all very
different and do not all fit the mold that we've been told to expect.
Not all are highly polished. Not all are trim and slim. Not all exude
the sizzle that you might expect.

I've observed the same as I've studied the women CEOs of the F500
and other executive women. They are different races and religions,
Democrats and Republicans and from varied family and economic
backgrounds. Some like team sports, others individual activities. Their
looks are different. Their styles are different. Not all have carefully
coiffed hair. Not all have manicured nails. Not all dress according
to a formula. As a matter of fact, Meg Whitman has said of herself
that no one would call her "fashion forward."

What *do* they have in common? Beyond the achievements that got them to the top, they know the business of their businesses and speak the language of power. When they're at the top of their games, they're articulate and confident. They're able to effectively engage key stakeholders inside and outside the company. And they have what I call "leadership presence" — they carry themselves in a way that enables them to draw and hold attention. So, what is leadership presence and what should you do to cultivate or enhance yours?

Unlike many pundits, I'm not going to tell you that leadership presence is about your attire — how you dress, the shoes you wear, your makeup or your hair — although, appearance does matter. You're already smart enough to dress to match the level to which you aspire, to avoid sexy/provocative clothes and to dress in alignment with the culture of your organization. Right? And, really, how many of the men above you (at least those outside of the fashion industry), will know if you're wearing shoes or suits by the latest designers? (The women above you might, but that's another matter.)

Because **leadership presence is the ability to credibly draw and hold attention, it's prerequisite for engaging and aligning others.** Leadership presence has three elements:

1. The Language of Power — what you say
2. The Power of Language — how you say it
3. Non-verbal Messages — how you carry yourself and what you do

The Language of Power

We've already spent many chapters on "what you say." To have something worthy to say, speak the language of outcomes. Hone your business, strategic and financial acumen. Add a heaping portion of professional expertise. Do your homework. Add a pinch of commentary on current events to the mix and you'll have something worth saying.

This chapter will focus on "how you say it," how you mine the power of language to make sure that what you say about the business is heard. In the next chapter we'll focus on non-verbal presence — how you carry yourself and what you do.

The Power of Language

Having something worthy to say is of little use if you can't draw attention and respect when you speak. Imagine how her boss would respond to this statement made by Tonya.

> "I, uh, umm, you know. You might not think this is such a good idea...I'm not sure I have fully thought this through. Um, maybe John should weigh in on it. But, anyway, if we reduce waste by 50%, it will have a positive effect. What I mean is that we might be able to increase our margin by 10% through lower cost of raw materials and cost of waste disposal. Or at least, upon due consideration, that's kinda what I think."

Ouch!

Why is this statement (whether spoken or written) so painful? There are two obvious problems. Tonya uses too many fillers and she discounts her message.

Fillers are the "ums," "ahs" and "you knows" that we use to fill dead air. If you listen to CEOs when they are being interviewed, you'll hear that the best use no fillers. When they aren't sure what the right next word is, they stay silent...and you should, too. Fillers are distracting and boring and draw attention away from the point you want to make.

Tonya has totally discounted her central and credible idea by telegraphing that the idea might not be good, hasn't been thought through and could be more credibly presented by John. Like Tonya, you might use discounting phrases like these:

- "You're probably not going to like this idea" (then they won't).
- "This might not be such a good idea" (they'll be prepared to think it isn't).
- "This might, possibly, kind of, perhaps, maybe, sort of work" (they'll think you aren't behind the idea).
- "You'll probably disagree" (yup, they'll try their best to, or patronizingly support it to protect your feelings).

- "This probably won't work" (they'll sure try to prove that it won't).
- "I'm just new" (you've handed them an excuse to not take you seriously).

These phrases are self-limiting and discounting. Sadly, they're frequently heard from women. To be taken seriously, don't use them.

On the opposite end of the spectrum, be wary of using too many intensifiers. Words like *very, great, super, excellent, really, "LOVE it!"* and the intensifier that I personally favor — *awesome* — magnify the message and when overused can make you come across as phony. If everything is always great, super or excellent, how can people trust your ability to intelligently evaluate?

Fillers and discounts leave listeners responding to Tonya as if she were talking from the outside — metaphorically she indicates that she does not belong in the conversation. Imagine if, instead, she had said,

> "At our last meeting, Jane offered the idea of reducing waste. Building on her idea, I conducted an analysis using information from the CFO. I discovered that if we reduce waste by 50%, we'll increase our margin by 10% through lower cost of raw materials and waste disposal."

This statement conveys greater leadership presence. Metaphorically, Tonya indicates that she's right in the center of things. How? Because she is using the language of power AND the power of language.

The language of power means she is speaking to cash, growth, return and/or customer. She:

1. Conducted a return on investment analysis.
2. Is speaking about increased return (increase margin by 10%).

The power of language means she:

1. Takes the floor and builds on what someone else said. This helps build team cohesion.

2. Uses an "I" statement. Instead of saying or writing things like, "we," "people," "everyone," she states her point, idea or concern by saying "*I* discovered..." This lets her stand out, be visible and take credit for her accomplishment.

3. Establishes credibility for her analysis by citing the source of the information.

4. Offers a direct statement with an important business solution.

5. Isn't abrasive or personal. She lets the information stand on its own merits.

6. Delivers a focused message that isn't vague or lost in surrounding fluff.

7. Makes a statement instead of asking a question.

These seven are among the key elements of the power of language. They contribute to your ability to command and hold attention. Other elements include:

Voice: speak with clear diction, audible level and not too high a pitch. This is a particular challenge for women whose tone tends to be higher than men (try singing "Happy Birthday," your speaking voice should be at the same tone as the first syllable "Hap"). Don't raise your voice at the end of a statement (a linguistic pattern that connotes doubt).

Avoid Qualifiers: Words like: *some, kind of, just, sort of, maybe,* and *perhaps* are usually unnecessary and lessen the clarity and impact of a comment. Instead of saying (or writing), "here are some ideas for you to consider," a stronger statement would be, "I propose three alternatives for you to consider."

Gain Attention with Preparatory Phrases

A few years ago, I read research that validated what we've always thought to be true: Men's minds are frequently in the gutter...or on the battlefield. Dr. Rachel Gur and her husband, both from the

University of Pennsylvania, studied which parts of women's and men's brains are active at different times. One of their conclusions:

> *"Even when studied at rest...men activate more primitive parts of the limbic system that do not have access to language, whereas women activate parts of the limbic system that are adjacent to language areas."*

What does this mean? As Ronna Lichtenberg writes in *Pitch Like a Girl*,

> *"...men, when left to their own devices for half an hour, are probably... thinking about sex or aggression...So now you know not to offer men a penny for their thoughts when they're resting — it's a 50/50 chance the answer is either sex or aggression."*

I reiterated this finding to one of my leadership classes. The next month, Noreen returned and in front of the entire class reported, "After the last class, I went home and told my husband what you said about men's minds frequently being on sex or on aggression. You know what he said?"

I sat quietly and a bit nervous half expecting to hear that he had vehemently disagreed with the finding. She went on, "He said, 'Yeah. Isn't it funny how that happens?'"

Needless to say, the entire class cracked up. But I had shared the research to make this very serious point. To command attention when you speak to men, you might have to attract their attention BEFORE making your point.

Women's failure to do this is one of the reasons that things we say in meetings are often not heard. We'll pop into a discussion, make an important point, and no one responds. Later, when a man makes the same exact point, he gets praise and credit for it. So, to avoid this problem, I advise the judicious use of what I call *preparatory phrases*. Men use them all the time! Here are five examples:

1. Bob, this is something that you're going to want to know...
2. Jerome, as you know from past discussions, the most important aspect of this situation is...
3. Mike, the most important thing to keep in mind at the moment is...
4. Jack, the action that is going to make all the difference here is...
5. Armando, you've asked a really good question. Let me tell you what I think about it...

These work for two reasons. First, you are using the person's name to grab attention. Second, you are speaking for a second or two without making your main point. This gives men time to shift their attention to what you say. You are preparing them to hear your point.

The next time you're in a meeting, pay attention to the preparatory phrases that you hear and see which seem to work in your culture. Then, take the opportunity to use them when you make a point that you want to be heard.

Madeleine Albright, former U.S. Secretary of State, advocates that you "Speak up!" and I agree. Speaking up will serve you best when you combine the language of power with the power of language. But that's not the whole equation for leadership presence. It's also about how you carry yourself — your non-verbal presence. We'll tackle that in the next chapter.

▶ Lead ON!

Document Review
Review your own or ask a trusted colleague or coach to review a selection of your written communication (especially e-mails), for elements of the power of language such as your use of the language of power, "I" statements, verbosity, qualifiers, intensifiers, exclamation points, etc.

Coaching Feedback

Ask a trusted colleague, mentor or coach to observe you in conversation and provide feedback on ways your use of language diminishes your credibility — or enhances it.

Power of Language Assessment

If you'd like to enlist the assistance of others in observing and giving feedback about how you use the power of language, go to *www. NoCeilingNoWalls.com* where you'll find the **Power of Language Assessment** tool. Print it out and give it to a trusted colleague, mentor or coach.

Tap the Power of Non-Verbals

"That elusive 'it' quality shared by great leaders throughout history. The way they walk onto a stage as though they belong there, or into a room as if everyone is a friend. They look you in the eye…they come off as strong, confident and in control…"

—Sarah Woods
writing for Bates Communication

Cultivating leadership presence means speaking the language of power (what you say), mining the power of language (how you say it) and presenting a non-verbal presence that says "leader" (how you carry yourself).

Let's revisit Tonya to see why non-verbals are so important. Imagine that Tonya has just bumped into her boss. Which posture (described on the right) best matches her statement?

"At our last meeting, Jane offered the idea of reducing waste. Building on her idea, I conducted an analysis using information from the CFO. I discovered that if we reduce waste by 50%, we'll increase our margin by 10% through lower cost of raw materials and waste disposal."	A. Tonya is standing with shoulders slumped as if she were carrying the weight of the world. Her folio is grasped tightly in front of her chest, her eyes are downcast, her head tilted to one side and she's shifting her weight from foot to foot. Her eyes nervously shift between her boss and the floor. B. Tonya is standing upright, her weight balanced evenly on both feet. She is directly facing her boss. Her head is level and she maintains eye contact.

The Tonya of the strong statement is the Tonya of the "B" non-verbals. The "A" non-verbals better fit the Tonya of fillers and discounts. Imagine for a minute her boss' reaction if she made the strong statement with the "weak" non-verbals. Chances are the boss wouldn't take Tonya seriously. Why? Because when there's a disconnect between what you say and how you appear, people believe what they see over what they hear. So, if you're verbalizing great ideas, but your posture, eye contact and gestures are self-protective and/or unsure, people won't take you seriously. That's why effective leaders align confident words with a confident non-verbal presence.

A confident non-verbal presence is comprised of three ingredients:
1. The belief that you're worthy of being paid attention to.
2. Non-verbal behaviors that communicate that you're worth listening to.
3. How you execute your leadership responsibilities.

Belief in Self-Worth

The belief that you're worthy of commanding and holding attention rests in part on your level of knowledge and experience. If you're a novice in your profession, you might believe that you are less worthy of speaking up than an expert. But on another level, feelings of self-worth are independent of expertise. Women are on the receiving end of messages that undermine self-worth. Consider: "Little girls should be seen, but not heard." "She's nothing but a pretty face." "Dumb blonde." "She's just a trophy wife." These and similar messages downplay women's competence, credibility and confidence.

To enhance feelings of self-worth, examine your programming to identify messages that might be undermining you. By becoming aware of them, you can shift your mindset and replace them with more functional messages. You can also test out an idea before you present it at a meeting — present it to a couple of co-workers and ask for their feedback.

Non-Verbal Presentation

You can tackle posture, eye contact and gestures directly with a "fake it until you make it" strategy and reinforce a virtuous confidence-building cycle. In the U.S., the ingredients of insecure non-verbals compared with the confident non-verbals are:

You Non-Verbally Communicate *Lack of Confidence* When You...	You Non-Verbally Communicate *Self-Confidence* When You...
Adopt a self-protective posture: slouch, bow your head, round your shoulders to protect your heart chakra. Metaphorically, you're ashamed or afraid.	Adopt an open posture: stand or sit straight and tall, heart chakra open, head held high.
Stand with your legs crossed at the ankle, or with all weight on one leg/hip. Metaphorically, you're off balance.	Stand with weight centered on two feet firmly on the ground.
Tilt your head to one side (metaphorically, offering your jugular is a sign of submission).	Face straight ahead.
Hand wringing, fidgeting gestures, upper arms hugged to the torso, arms crossed, hands clasped behind your back.	Use gestures aligned with what you're saying, neither overly exaggerated nor constrained.
Shift eyes, avoiding eye contact.	Use appropriate eye contact. Neither aggressively boring in on someone, nor staring off into space.
Nod if you disagree. Women often nod to indicate, "I hear you." Men interpret this as agreement.	Maintain a neutral facial expression as you listen to something you disagree with.
Smile away bad news.	Deliver bad news with the facial solemnity it deserves.

The behaviors on the left can diminish your leadership presence no matter the value of what you say, so rev up your credibility by making sure that your non-verbal communication reflects the behaviors on the right.

What about non-verbal presence in the virtual world? When people can't see you, they make assumptions about you based on other observable patterns of behavior. Is your business e-mail full of emoticons, cute backgrounds and flash cartoons? If so, stop. Do you come across on social networking sites as a thought leader or accomplished professional; or do you come across as a partying lightweight sharing articles and blogs on fashion and diet?

To ratchet up your "thought leader" presence, forward industry news not the latest cute story. If you comment on blogs, make your comments thoughtful. Get on LinkedIn, not just your college social networking site. When you use Twitter, think about what you share. The first dozen Tweets of a college senior I know were complaints about her job on the yearbook — not a very professional image to present to a prospective hiring manager who might check her out.

Whether in person or in the virtual world, be sure that you center yourself in your strongest place and present yourself with confidence.

Executing Leadership Responsibilities

Not only is leadership presence conveyed by non-verbal presentation, it is also communicated through leadership actions. As discussed in the chapter Leadership Is Gender Neutral, women face a double bind when it comes to developing our leadership styles. When we act in concert with stereotypes about women, we are seen as weak. When we act off-stereotype, we are considered hard and aggressive. Robert Kabacoff reported on a study by the Management Research Group, *"Male CEOs and senior vice-presidents got high marks from their bosses when they were forceful and assertive and lower scores if they were cooperative and empathic. The opposite was true for women. Female CEOs got downgraded for being assertive and got better scores when they were cooperative."*

John O'Rourke, who hired Angela Braly into RightCHOICE (eventually acquired by WellPoint), illustrates this. He has described Angela this way, *"I like to characterize her as soccer mom on one hand and Napoleonic soldier on the other."* Why didn't he simply say that she's a very effective executive?

Contrast O'Rourke's comment with how noted business expert and author Ram Charan describes Ellen Kullman, CEO of DuPont, *"She is very conversant on what is happening in the market and with customers on a worldwide basis. The businesses she has been accountable for have given her insight into the needs of customers in China, India, Brazil, Europe, and Russia. Looking at the future, the great growth will come from these countries."*

It's important for women to develop a style that is both "take charge" *and* "take care," that demonstrates both business acumen *and* interpersonal skills, that uses both compliance strategies *and* engagement strategies, that's decisive *and* participative.

Michelle Bachelet, president of Chile, describes this challenge when she says, *"I have made a conscious choice that I will pursue a leadership style that can be strong and authoritative but retain 'womanly attributes'...That is why I push for social dialogue, because I think the best thing for the economy and the people is for everyone — owners, managers and workers — to sit down and see how we can move forward together. When developing the latest pension system reform, for example, I set up a commission of intellectuals and practical people — those with know-how and different political perspectives. Many people laughed and said it was because I was unable to make decisions. They were completely wrong."* To execute her leadership responsibilities in a way that would include both, she "took care" through a commission that gave voice to experts and citizens, and she "took charge" of reforming Chile's pension system.

Meg Whitman, former CEO of eBay, clearly understands that she has to strike a balance between engagement and action. She says, *"You have to make decisions. What will kill a growth company is someone who can't make decisions. But you have to listen very hard, recognize which constituencies are speaking and then make a decision for the greater good."* And, Lynn Elsenhans, CEO of Sunoco, describes it this way, *"Research shows that women leaders tend to be either competent or liked, but rarely both, and that's a double bind. People don't tend to trust people they don't like, and it's very hard in business to lead if there isn't mutual trust and respect. It's also difficult to go forward in a company if you're not considered competent."*

So what should a woman do? First, recognize that you can't control other people's reactions to you. You can only control your behaviors, so be:

1. Competent: Know (and be straightforward about) what you know, know what you're expected to know and know what you don't know.

2. Trustworthy: Denise Nemchev, Staff Executive of Complex Management for Stanley Works, advises, *"Build teams based on trust, make and meet commitments, establish a high "say/do" ratio."* In other words, do what you say you're going to do many more times than not.

3. Respectful: Approach each person with the belief that s/he has greatness within and fundamentally wants to do a good job.

4. Open: Lynn Elsenhans says, *"One of the hardest lessons for me to learn as a leader was the need to give up being right. If you're always advocating your position, you aren't being open to the ideas of others."* Strike a balance between advocacy and inquiry.

5. Assertive, not aggressive: How do you tell the difference? Assertiveness is about "we" and aggression is about "I."

What do you communicate non-verbally when you execute your leadership actions? Do you look like a dictator because you never utilize forums for collecting input from others or do you create such forums as Kimball Hall, VP and general manager of Amgen, does. One of Kimball's goals for her team is robust dialogue. As the new site manager, she used tools of role-shifting to stimulate discussion within a team that wasn't accustomed to being asked for input. To promote dialogue and encourage staff to think cross-functionally, she asked her direct reports to take on different functional and attitudinal roles when discussing important issues. For example, she'd ask her HR Director to take on the role of the Operations Manager; or she'd ask someone who is usually a cheerleader for new ideas to take on the role of the naysayer.

Do you always sit at the head of the table when you're running a meeting, do you never sit at the head or do you sometimes sit in the center as Carol Smith, SVP and chief brand officer for of Elle Group, does? *"I don't instantly sit at the head of the table. I sit in the middle of the table...I want to be part of the process and part of the decision."*

When you walk the halls, do you walk with purpose and disregard those around you or do you walk with purpose and have time to say a brief "hello"? Do you hurry as if you're overburdened by too much to do, or do you walk as if you are the master of your time?

Why are these important to consider? Because when you're in a position of leadership, the way you carry yourself and everything you do is magnified. Be intentional about what you communicate non-verbally. No matter your level, make sure that you communicate confidence, competence and credibility.

Leadership presence is about drawing and holding attention through what you say, how you say it and what you do. As Carol Smith says, *"I know when I walk into a room of employees, I command a presence."* You demonstrate leadership presence at staff meetings and onstage. You begin to cultivate leadership presence as an individual contributor and must hone it as you move up the organization.

▶ Lead ON!

Leadership Presence Feedback

Give our **Leadership Presence Feedback Tool** (found at *www. NoCeilingNoWalls.com*) to a trusted colleague, mentor or manager and ask for feedback on your leadership presence. Ask for feedback on your behavior in meetings — it is useful whether you are facilitating the meeting or are a contributing member, whether you're making a formal presentation or informally participating.

Leadership Presence @ Every Level

At the **individual contributor** level, take advantage of any opportunity to present at a staff meeting or to take company-sponsored presentation skills courses. With a growth mindset in place, ask for, be receptive to and take action on feedback about how you come across. The Leadership Presence feedback tool can help you shape the feedback you request.

As a **manager,** you'll not only be expected to have mastered leadership presence for internal communication but also for external venues. Create or take advantage of opportunities to speak at industry or professional forums. Courses like Dale Carnegie or working with a speech coach can help you develop comfort with public speaking.

As an **executive,** it will be important to receive media training as you take advantage of opportunities presented by your communications department to be a company spokesperson. Support your company's internal women's network by presenting your career path and leadership lessons to women who are more junior.

At the **board** level, you want to avoid taking on one of the problem personas described by Bev Behan of Board Advisor, LLC:
- Pit bull — an overly aggressive and combative director whose questions sound accusatory rather than inquisitive.
- Management lapdog — someone who always sides with management, lets them off the hook when tough issues might create problems for the CEO.
- Checked-out — the director who arrives unprepared, late, and is disengaged (except to lob in an off-the-wall comment).

Enhance Your Leadership Presence
- Take advantage of any opportunity you have to be videotaped and use the **Leadership Presence Feedback Tool** to assess how you come across.
- Observe yourself as you go through your work day. Ask what messages about your leadership are delivered

by what you do every day. For example, do you walk around looking frazzled and overwhelmed, or cool as a cucumber? Do you look indecisive because you never represent yourself as making a decision?

- Take an objective look at your office/work space — what does it say about you as a leader? What's the balance between cute calendars, family photos and executive toys, and/or business books, performance charts, awards and certificates? What about your work space says "leader" and what could you change to reinforce the message?

- Monitor your online/virtual presence — or ask a trusted colleague or coach to Google your name and take an objective look at your online presence. What could you change in order to appear professional, competent and credible?

WATCH Leading Women

Learn from credible role models. For links to speeches by Patricia Woertz, CEO Archer Daniels Midland, and Ursula Burns, CEO of Xerox, that illustrate key points about leadership presence, go to *www.NoCeilingNoWalls.com* and download the related guides that point out key strengths for each speech.

Create *Your* No Ceiling, No Walls Career

"When I dare to be powerful — to use my strength in the service of my vision, then it comes less and less important whether I am afraid."
—AUDRE LORDE

You've been called to leadership. Whether the call comes from within you or through a tap on the shoulder, the call is an awesome responsibility and an incredible honor. It puts in your hands the power to make a positive difference in the lives of co-workers, colleagues, direct reports, customers, those you report to and anyone else you touch in the course of a workday.

I invite you and encourage you to heed the call.

I hope the lessons within these pages have kindled or rekindled your passion for leadership. With these lessons and examples, your path to success has been strengthened because you:

- Live an understanding that "leadership is using the greatness in you to achieve and sustain extraordinary outcomes by engaging the greatness in others."
- Understand how the *whys* of leadership will help you become a wise leader.

- Fill the Missing 33%, knock the socks off of those who *perceive* women to have less business, strategic and financial acumen and close the biggest potential gap in your success equation.
- See aspects of yourself in the trailblazing leading women who have served as your virtual mentors.
- Speak the Language of Power without losing your voice.
- Cultivate your own greatness while engaging it in others.
- Use the Lead ON! tools (and those on our website) to enhance your capacity to lead.
- Escape the box (glass ceiling, maternal walls and sticky floor) to enjoy career success — however you define it.

I hope *No Ceiling, No Walls* helps you feel emboldened to seize this power and to answer your call to leadership with the unique greatness that is yours alone to bring.

It's an honor to share your leadership journey with you, and I wish you no ceiling to your ambitions and no walls to close you in!

Lead ON!

Susan L. Colantuono
Green Hill Beach, RI
Paradise Valley, MT

Recommended Reading

Great resources for further exploration of leadership and what women need to know about leadership from career-start to the corporate boardroom:

Use Personal Greatness
- *True North* by Bill George
- *Authentic Leadership* by Bill George
- *Know How* by Ram Charan
- *Mindset: The Psychology of Success* by Carol Dweck
- *On Becoming a Leader* by Warren Bennis
- *Power Talk* by Sarah Myers McGinty
- *The Five Temptations of a CEO* by Patrick Lencioni
- *The Four Obsessions of an Extraordinary Executive* by Patrick Lencioni

Achieve Outcomes
- *What the CEO Wants You to Know* by Ram Charan
- *Profitable Growth is Everyone's Business* by Ram Charan
- *Execution* by Larry Bossidy and Ram Charan
- *Blue Ocean Strategy* by W. Chan Kim and Renee Mauborgne
- *Confronting Reality* by Larry Bossidy and Ram Charan
- *Good to Great and the Social Sectors* by Jim Collins
- *Good to Great* by Jim Collins

- *Mavericks at Work* by William C. Taylor and Polly LaBarre
- *The Game-Changer* by A. G. Lafley and Ram Charan
- *Building Better Boards* by David Nadler and Bev Behan
- *The Board Book: An Insiders Guide for Directors and Trustees* by William G. Bowen

Engage the Greatness in Others
- *Difficult Conversations* by Stone, et al.
- *Fierce Conversations* by Susan Scott
- *Her Place at the Table* by Kolb, et al.
- *Love is the Killer App* by Tim Sanders
- *Pitch Like a Girl* by Ronna Lichtenberg
- *Women Don't Ask* by Linda Babcock and Sara Laschever

On Women and Leadership
- *Her Turn* by Vicki Donlan
- *It's Not a Glass Ceiling, It's a Sticky Floor* by Rebecca Shambaugh
- *Katharine Graham* by Robin Gerber
- *Leadership the Eleanor Roosevelt Way* by Robin Gerber
- *Madam Secretary* by Madeleine Albright
- *Personal History* by Katharine Graham
- *Tough Choices* by Carly Fiorina
- *The Martha Rules* by Martha Stewart

On Career Success
- *Be Your Own Mentor* by Sheila Wellington/Catalyst
- *Getting Even* by Evelyn Murphy
- *I Didn't See it Coming* by Widmann, et al.
- *Play Like a Man, Win Like a Woman* by Gail Evans
- *She Wins, You Win* by Gail Evans
- *Nice Girls Don't Get the Corner Office* by Lois P. Frakel
- *Right from the Start: Taking Charge in a New Leadership Role* by Dan Ciampa and Michael Watkins
- *Womenomics* by Claire Shipman and Katty Kay

Challenging Ideas from Thought Leaders
*   *Managers Not MBAs* by Henry Mintzberg
*   *The Future of Management* by Gary Hamel
*   *Searching for a Corporate Savior: The Irrational Quest for Charismatic CEOs* by Rakesh Khurana

Acknowledgements

My personal lessons in leadership have been possible because of the thousands of colleagues, clients and friends with whom I've worked during my career. There are too many to name, but I owe particular gratitude to my first boss, Dave Chichester, and CEO Henry Roberts, who gave me a powerful and positive career-start.

Annette Cerilli of the Bryant University Executive Development Center first saw the need for my definition and model of leadership and supported my launch of the Women's Institute for Leadership at Bryant.

Jane Metzger, Kathleen Hittner and other amazing women executives and managers at Lifespan were role models for and shared lessons about leadership in health care. My former colleagues at the Lifespan Learning Institute created a supportive environment for the launch of its Center for Leadership Excellence.

For the deeply rewarding journey that is Leading Women, profound thanks to Lisa Bergeron, president of SENE, and Victoria Waterman, president of MASS, and all of our amazing and inspiring clients.

In the creation of this book, I am especially grateful for the assistance of these consummate professionals:

My editor, the amazing and inspirational Juli Baldwin of the Baldwin Group. With clarity and care, Juli set me on the right track more than once.

Graham van Dixhorn and Susan Kendrick of Write to Your Market for the consultative approach, category-of-one title and motivating back copy.

The creative Michele DeFilippo of 1106 Design for the arresting cover and interior design.

Fred Macri, EVP of Lifespan, and Ann Kashmanian, CPA and VP of Finance at Rhode Island Hospital, for review of the chapter on financial acumen.

And the scores of Leading Women members who've helped refine the content and whose responses to my e-mails and surveys shaped the title, subtitle and cover design!

Continue to Build *Your* No Ceiling, No Walls Career

Become a more confident, inspired and effective leader. *Leading Women's* diverse services and resources, created *for women and by women,* support your success from career-start to the C-suite and onto corporate boards.

1. **Live Leadership Programs**

   These inspiring, informative and engaging multi-session programs offer content specific to the demands of leaders @ every level. From our Ready, Set, LEAD™ program for emerging leaders to our Women on Boards™ program for executive women, you'll find the program that is just what you need to power your success.

   www.LeadingWomen.biz/Leadership

2. **Virtual Leadership Solutions**

   Can't make it to our live programs? You can still support your career aspirations with the same unique and innovative content. Invest in a GOLD Membership to gain access to our **ASK** Leading women online resources. These include teleseminars, multimedia programming, interviews with thought leaders, authors and executives; and more.

   www.LeadingWomen.biz/Join

3. Mentor/Protégé Program

Are you looking for a mentor to help you hone your business acumen, ability to engage others or build a strategic network; could you benefit from a mentor in another company...or a mentor at a higher level within your profession? Your GOLD Membership also provides the opportunity to find a mentor who can fit these or many other criteria.
www.LeadingWomen.biz/GOLD

If you'd like to send comments or questions or want to receive advance information on upcoming books in the ASK Leading Women™ series, e-mail me: *Susan.Colantuono@LeadingWomen.biz.*

Advance and Retain Women! — Solutions for Organizations

Advance, Retain — Results! Overcome the common barriers to women's advancement with our uncommon solutions designed for diversity and learning and development departments and women's networks. *Leading Women's* live, online and Self-Managed Solutions™ provide the career-advancing skills and knowledge that women need in these areas, including:

1. **Leadership**
   Close the most crucial gaps between typical leadership development programs and the leadership skills that women need in order to move up. You'll see positive results from our interactive, engaging, and practical programs for leaders @ every level. *www.LeadingWomen.biz/Leadership*

2. **Mentoring**
   There are three elements missing from most traditional mentoring programs. You'll need them to ensure the success of your mentoring program or to launch an effective one. To talk about these three elements and other mentoring success criteria, give us a call at 401-789-0441.

3. **Strategic Networking**

   Embed the nine critical networking skills that enable women to leverage internal and external strategic relationships for business and career success. Find out what they are and how to offer them to your women.

   Email us: *info@leadingwomen.biz*

4. **Corporate Boards**

   Our cutting-edge Women on Boards™ program prepares women executives for director positions on corporate boards.
   www.LeadingWomen.biz/WOB

Think these topics sound familiar? We guarantee that our approaches are unique. For more information, visit: *www.LeadingWomen.biz/ Advance.*

Strengthen your Internal Women's Initiative, Network or affinity group (IWiN) through:

1. **IWiN Strategic Alignment**

   Whether you're starting an initiative or planning future activities, Leading Women will help you ensure relevance, alignment with business goals and measurable positive results. Read about our clients' successes: *www.LeadingWomen.biz/Cases.*

2. **IWiN Leadership Development**

   Cultivate leadership skills, plan for succession and develop future IWiN leaders with Leading Women's Self-Managed Solutions™, IWiN Conferences, IWiN newsletters and consultation.

To discover the many ways that Leading Women can help your organization advance and retain women, call for a free 30-minute consultation at 401-789-0441.

About the Author

When Susan Colantuono was 16 months old, her brother was born, thus launching a lifelong interest in gender dynamics and an abundance of heretical observations and breakthrough thinking about women, leadership and careers.

With a clarion call to leaders and practical advice about purpose, power and presence, Susan's no-nonsense and comprehensive insights guide women to more inspired and confident leadership...and more fulfilling careers. As testament to the power of her message, over three quarters of the women who have taken her programs achieve their goals of promotions or increased responsibility.

Susan shares her wisdom as CEO of Leading Women, where she inspires and powers the success of women leaders in organizations and through her writings. Her most recent book, *No Ceiling, No Walls: What women haven't been told about leadership from career-start to the corporate boardroom,* has been described as a "must read" by CEOs and thought leaders alike.

Susan is the founder of the Women's Institute for Leadership at Bryant University in Smithfield, R.I., past director of the Rhode Island State Council of the Society for Human Resource Management (SHRM) and has been honored by *Providence Business News* as Ally and Mentor for Business Women. She loves her family, the south of France, horse camping in Yellowstone and Lindt Excellence 85% Cocoa Bars...not necessarily in that order.